WORLD'S GREATEST AIRL

CW01237865

THE VICKERS VISCOUNT

THE WORLD'S FIRST TURBOPROP AIRLINE

WORLD'S GREATEST AIRLINERS

THE VICKERS VISCOUNT

THE WORLD'S FIRST TURBOPROP AIRLINE

NICK STROUD

First published in Great Britain in 2018
by Frontline Boooks
An imprint of Pen & Sword Books Limited
47 Church Street
Barnsley
South Yorkshire
S70 2AS

Copyright © Nick Stroud

ISBN 9781526701954

The right of Nick Stroud to be identified as
Author of this work has been asserted by him/her in accordance
with the Copyright, Designs and Patents Act 1988.
A CIP catalogue record for this book is
available from the British Library
All rights reserved. No part of this book may be reproduced or
transmitted in any form or by any means, electronic or mechanical
including photocopying, recording or by any information storage and
retrieval system, without permission from the Publisher in writing.

Typeset by Paul Wilkinson

Printed and bound in India
by Replika Press Pvt Ltd.

Pen & Sword Books Limited incorporates the imprints of Atlas,
Archaeology, Aviation, Discovery, Family History, Fiction, History, Maritime, Military, Military Classics, Politics,
Select, Transport, True Crime, Air World, Frontline Publishing, Leo Cooper, Remember When, Seaforth Publishing,
The Praetorian Press, Wharncliffe Local History, Wharncliffe Transport,
Wharncliffe True Crime and White Owl.

For a complete list of Pen & Sword titles please contact
PEN & SWORD BOOKS LIMITED
47 Church Street, Barnsley, South Yorkshire, S70 2AS, United Kingdom
E-mail: enquiries@pen-and-sword.co.uk
Website: www.pen-and-sword.co.uk

Contents

Introduction

BORN WHEN MY late father, Mike Stroud, was putting together the first issue of British magazine *Aircraft Illustrated* as one of its founding Editors, I was brought into the world with the sound of aero-engines in my ears. Indeed, family folklore maintains that the ear-splitting appearance of four McDonnell Douglas Phantoms at Farnborough during my first air display, when I was six months old, wreaked permanent damage on those tender little lugholes. Spending as much time as my aviation journalist father and I did around aircraft in my pre-primary school years, it became a matter of some consideration between us in what type I would first take to the air. For me, it had to be the USAF's Convair B-58 Hustler supersonic delta-winged Cold War bomber. As this looked unlikely in the UK in the early 1970s, we started thinking about alternatives, and I was delighted when, for my upcoming birthday, it had been arranged that the family would fly to Strasbourg in north-eastern France for a few days.

And so it was that on Thursday, February 27, 1974, my sixth birthday, we made our way to Heathrow to fly on British Midland Airways' twice-weekly Viscount service to the picturesque town on the French-German border. It was to be my first flight and I was therefore allowed to take the window seat; and what windows they were! About the same size as me, these massive ovals offered an unsurpassed view, particularly if you were seated aft of the wing – which we were. My excitement knew no bounds as the Rolls-Royce Dart turboprops of BMA Viscount 813 G-AZNA spooled up into their characteristic high-pitched whine. Rumbling over the tarmac towards the runway, where we lined up on the "piano keys", was beyond thrilling. Watching the runway fall away below through the gigantic windows after a short gallop down the runway was spellbinding, as was being above the clouds for the first time. The view was breathtaking through this magical looking-glass: with nose firmly pressed against the window I could see forward to the wing and its resolute Darts driving us on towards the Continent; isolated clusters of top-lit white cumulo-nimbus rolled by below; a glance up revealed the steadily deepening blue stretching away forever, and to the rear was the tip of the Viscount's distinctive upturned tailplane. I feel lucky to have had my first taste of flying aboard a type which made a virtue of emphasising the unique experience of air travel, especially in comparison to the uncomfortable sensory-deprivation-tank experience it often feels like today. The point of the Viscount was to enjoy the flight, not merely endure it.

So why the meander down memory lane? When Air World Editor Martin Mace approached me about the possibility of writing a book on a civil subject, he generously gave me a free hand when it came to choosing the subject. Without hesitation I said Viscount; it represents a "Great British Success Story", was produced in greater numbers than any other British medium-range airliner, and

Vickers Viscount 813 G-AZNA (c/n 350), seen here in its British Midland Airways (BMA) colour scheme, was originally built for South African Airways, and after making its maiden flight on December 7, 1958, was delivered on the 20th of that month. It joined BMA in March 1972, and was the aircraft in which the author, aged six, made his first flight in February 1974.
(The Aviation Historian Archive)

was operated by some 200 individual organisations in more than 80 countries over four decades – not bad for a type that was very nearly sidelined before a single airframe had been built. But more important than all these remarkable achievements for me was the fact that the Viscount had given me my first taste of flight back in 1974, and I've felt a strong kinship with it ever since. I've flown in numerous types since then, from Second World War bombers to military jets (although not a B-58 Hustler, sadly), but none hold as significant a place in my heart as the Viscount, still the most successful four-engined airliner in British aviation history.

VICKERS VISCOUNT V.701 G-AMAV

This cutaway drawing by R.E. Poulton of the prototype Viscount 700-series, V.701 G-AMAV, was first published in the September 7, 1950, issue of *Flight*, just a few weeks after the aircraft had made its first flight. The detail drawing at top left shows the aileron's flexible air-seal, which prevented air leaking from the underside to the topside of the wing. The middle-right detail drawing shows the double-slotted flaps at full deflection, and the system of operating them by means of a chain-and-sprocket link from a torque tube. The detail drawing at lower right shows the warm-air anti-icing airflow within the double skin on the wing's leading edge. (© Flightglobal 2018)

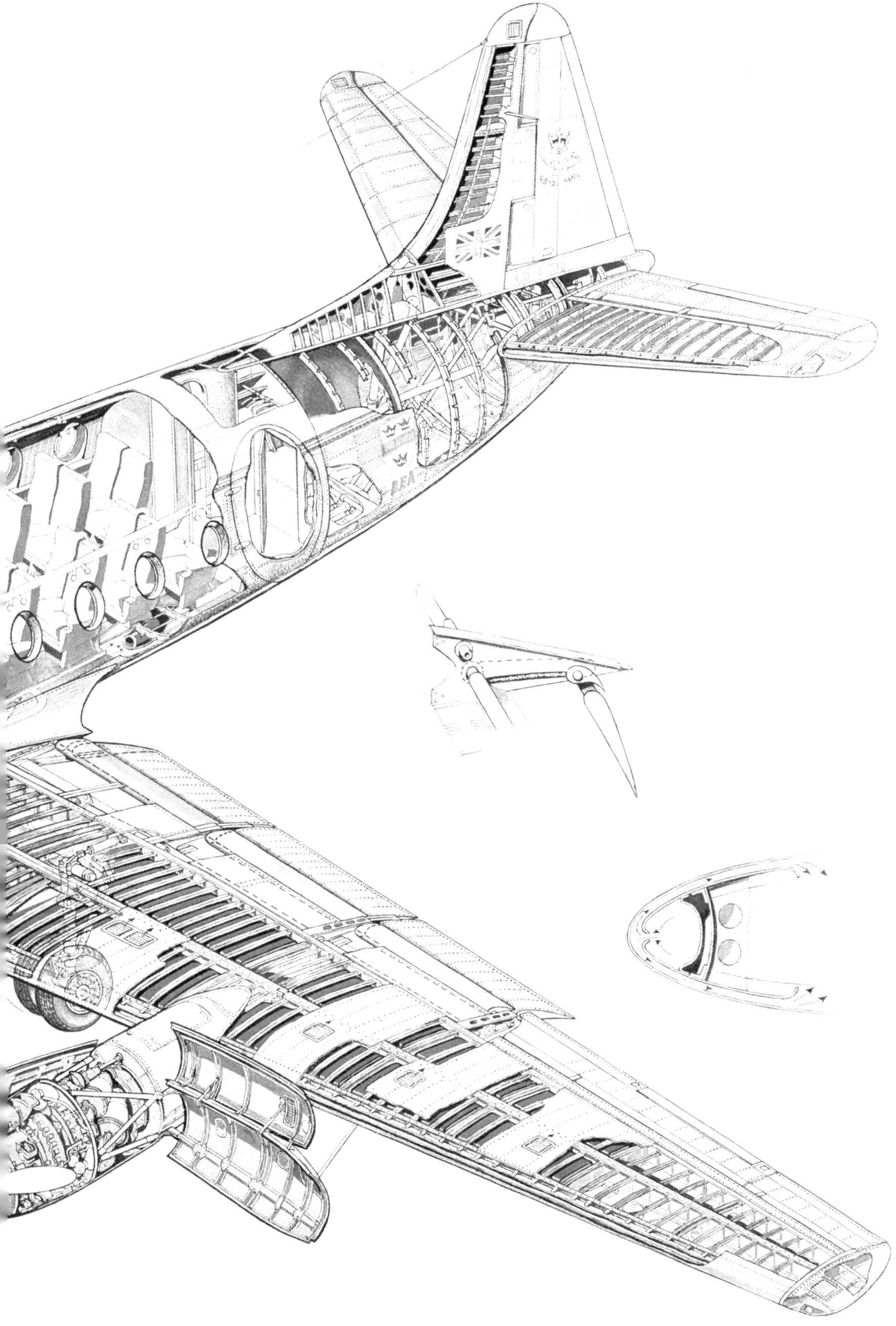

CHAPTER 1

Genesis

THE ORIGIN OF what would ultimately be one of the greatest success stories of Britain's post-war aircraft industry dates back to a resolutely optimistic appraisal undertaken by a committee convened in the dying days of 1942 to discuss what the nation's post-war civil aircraft needs might be – a bold course of action at a time when the successful conclusion of the war against the Axis powers was far from certain.

Although Britain had been responsible for some of the most successful civil aircraft of the pre-war period, the outbreak of war in Europe in 1939 had forced the redeployment of the nation's resources on to a war footing, the development of commercial aircraft having to be set aside in order to accommodate the mass production of warplanes for the impending conflict. This enormous acceleration in the production of fighters, bombers and other vital military types would, however, take some time to gather momentum, and in the interim Britain would be in desperate need of aircraft to bridge the gap. The nation's air arms had secured a temporary respite during the crucial Battle of Britain — but only by the narrowest of margins. Hard times were ahead, and to keep Britain's forces bolstered against those of Nazi Germany, the USA abandoned all pretence of impartiality, and in March 1941 enacted its Lend-Lease policy, in which food, oil and, importantly, military materiel would be supplied to nations facing the Axis war machine, most notably the UK. America was yet to become embroiled in the conflict and, in contrast to Britain, was still very much in the transport aircraft business; the USA would continue to develop civil types even after declaring war on Japan, Germany and Italy in December 1941. An important proviso of Lend-Lease, however, was that all materiel received was, on the cessation of hostilities, to be paid for in full, returned to the USA or destroyed. The thousands of transport aircraft received by the British as part of Lend-Lease, eminently convertible for commercial use, could not therefore be used as the backbone for the UK's post-war airline industry.

Aware of this prospective handicap and showing remarkable prescience, the British government established a committee in the autumn of 1942 to devise a post-war civil aviation strategy. It was to be led by Lord Brabazon of Tara, the first person in Britain to be awarded a Royal Aero Club Aviator's Certificate, in 1910, and formerly Minister of Transport during 1940–41 and Minister of Aircraft Production during 1941–42. Brabazon was tasked with organising an advisory committee to formulate plans for the procurement of suitable aircraft and the re-establishment of international air services, which, it was forecast, would continue operations over the pre-war routes to the furthest-flung reaches of the British Empire.

The first meeting of the Brabazon Committee was held on December 23, 1942, and was attended by Brabazon, three representatives from the Air Ministry and three from the Ministry of Aircraft Production, who over the next few months

Having first flown in December 1935, the Douglas DC-3 became ubiquitous in service with airlines all over the world, particularly after the Second World War, when the type became readily available from surplus military stocks, and at affordable prices for fledgling airlines. One of the chief specifications set out by the wartime British Brabazon Committee was for a homegrown DC-3 replacement that could serve the nation's post-war domestic and short-haul routes, and it was with this in mind that Vickers conceived what would eventually become the Viscount. (The Aviation Historian Archive)

would shape the basic template of requirements that the post-war civil aircraft industry would have to meet. A second committee was established in the spring of 1943 to dig deeper into detail, the eight-man panel comprising individuals from industry, the relevant ministries and the British Overseas Airways Corporation (BOAC). Mention had already been made by the first committee of "an economical [Douglas] DC-3 replacement for European services", and after a number of iterations discussed by the Brabazon Committee and the new Ministry of Civil Aviation, established in November 1944, this eventually metamorphosed into requirement IIB, a sub-section of the second of five types outlined in the Brabazon Committee's final report of 1945. Requirement II was for a medium-range 24-seat pressurised transport aircraft, the B suffix denoting that it was to be powered by four gas-turbine (turboprop) engines, a form of technology which at that time was untried and still very much in development, but which Vickers nevertheless felt showed a great deal of promise.

Originally designed to a 1932 specification for a long-range twin-engined bomber, the Vickers Wellington first flew in June 1936 and provided sterling service for the RAF throughout the Second World War, despite being obsolete in comparison to its younger four-engined service-mates, the Avro Lancaster and Handley Page Halifax. The type was nevertheless a great success for Vickers, more than 11,460 examples being built. It was the only RAF bomber to be produced for the duration of the war, and was one of the few types to be in front-line service both when war broke out in 1940 and when the war ended in 1945. (The Aviation Historian Archive)

One of the most important captains of Britain's post-war aviation industry, George (Sir George from 1957) Edwards joined Vickers at Weybridge as a draughtsman in 1935, rising to Experimental Works Manager in 1940 and Chief Designer in June 1945. He would go on to be responsible for the development of the highly successful Viscount airliner and Valiant V-bomber, and eventually became Vickers' Managing Director in 1955. He would also play an important part in the development of Concorde after Vickers became part of the British Aircraft Corporation in 1960. (The Aviation Historian Archive)

By mid-1944 Vickers had already seen the writing on the wall and started the development of the Vickers Commercial 1 (VC1), a civil development of its ageing but dependable Wellington twin-engined bomber, which had seen service since the first days of the war. The Wellington's distinctive geodetic fuselage construction was replaced with a more modern stressed-skin fuselage and inner-wing sections, but initially retained the geodetic fabric-covered outer wings and tailplane of its military progenitor. The first prototype Vickers V.491 VC1 Viking, registered G-AGOK, made its first flight on June 22, 1945, from the company's airfield at Wisley, and the first production V.498 Viking commenced operational trials with BOAC from May 1946.

With the Ministry of Aircraft Production's approval, Vickers then set to work on the IIB proposal, with an initial design forthcoming in June 1945 from the company's chief designer, R.K. "Rex" Pierson, who would be promoted Chief Engineer of Vickers-Armstrongs that September, George (later Sir George) Edwards filling his shoes thereafter. The June 1945 concept, designated VC2, incorporated a portly "double-bubble" pressurised fuselage seating 24 passengers three abreast, 88ft (26·8m)-span wings, a fin similar to that of the Viking and four Rolls-Royce Dart engines which it was anticipated would provide a cruising speed of some 300 m.p.h. (480km/h) over a range of more than 1,000 miles (1,609km). Although comparatively little of it would be retained in what would become one of the most distinctive shapes in British airliner history, the bones of the Viscount were already clearly visible in this early design.

The arrival of Edwards as chief designer in September 1945 led to a number of substantial changes to the VC2 design, including the replacement of the double-bubble fuselage with a more conventional circular-section design capable of accommodating four-abreast seating, wings of equal straight taper, a dihedral tailplane and generously proportioned elliptical cabin windows, all of which would be retained on all variants of the final product. Progress with the various turboprop powerplants being developed concurrently had slowed, however, and it was Armstrong Siddeley's Mamba that was selected by the Ministry of Supply (MoS) when it placed its official order for two prototype VC2s in March

Using the Wellington as a basic blueprint, Vickers' chief designer R.K. "Rex" Pierson initially retained the bomber's fabric-clad geodetic wing and tail unit to create the VC1 Viking, which incorporated a new metal fuselage capable of accommodating up to 24 passengers, although later versions had metal wings and empennages and could be configured for up to 36 passengers. Production stopped in 1948, by which time 163 examples of the piston-engined airliner had been built. (The Aviation Historian Archive)

(John Havers Collection via The Aviation Historian Archive)

1946 to Specification 8/46, although Vickers continued to pin its hopes on the Dart throughout the procurement process.

Another significant milestone was reached in August 1946 with the establishment of British European Airways (BEA), a nationalised corporation responsible for domestic and international short-haul air services, and the prime customer for the new Vickers turboprop, which was designated V.609 and named Viceroy that November. The new airline immediately began consultations with Vickers, stipulating that it estimated a requirement for 75 aircraft capable of carrying 32 passengers over short- to medium-haul routes, prompting further changes to the VC2, including increased span and length to accommodate more passengers, although the Mamba powerplants were retained. Vickers still advocated the use of the Dart, however, and in August 1946 elected to build, as a private venture, another prototype powered by the Rolls-Royce engine, although by August the following year the MoS had relented and authorised Vickers to build the original prototype with Darts, the manufacturer redesignating it V.630. A scheme was also put forward in which the type would be powered by a Dart in each inner engine nacelle and a Rolls-Royce Nene turbojet on each of the outers, but this expensive and unnecessarily complicated idea ultimately came to nothing.

August 1947 not only saw a change in powerplant for the new airliner, but a change in name too. The Partition of India was officially declared on August

Arguably more elegant than its turboprop-powered Vickers rival, the piston-engined triple-tailed Airspeed Ambassador first flew in July 1947 and entered service with British European Airways (BEA) as the "Elizabethan Class" in 1952. Pressurised and offering spectacular views for passengers by virtue of its high-mounted wing, the 45–50-seat Ambassador was initially extremely popular with the public, but the superior efficiency and speed of new turboprops like the Viscount ensured that only 23 examples were built, and the BEA fleet had been retired by the end of 1958. Other operators such as Dan-Air, Autair and BKS Air Transport were swift to snap up those that remained airworthy and some of these remained in service well into the 1960s, Dan-Air retiring its last remaining example in 1971. (The Aviation Historian Archive)

14–15, consigning the post of British Viceroy to history, and it was felt that the alternative name Viscount was similarly honourable and alliterative, and was adopted forthwith. By the end of 1947 the new Vickers design was shaping up into a sophisticated modern airliner, and the Dart engine was finally making good progress in its extensive flight-testing programme, which had started with its fitting in a number of test-beds from that October.

So it came as something of a hammer-blow when BEA indicated in December 1947 that it would be ordering 20 examples of the larger Airspeed Ambassador, designed to Brabazon requirement IIA, essentially the same as that of the Viscount, but with piston engines. Unsurprisingly, with no firm orders from any airline and a kick in the teeth from the company's biggest hope for its new airliner, Vickers' work on the Viscount slowed down to a dribble with the attendant effect on the team's morale. The new airline had repeatedly expressed its concern that the Vickers type was too small and presented too great a risk with its unproven Dart turboprops, resulting in a re-examination of the design in mid-1947 by Edwards, who came up with a number of revisions, including a larger wing carrying a pair of Bristol Hercules piston engines and a larger 40-seat version with four Darts, the Rolls-Royce engine having finally begun to fulfil its promise. Neither of these revised designs was approved by the MoS, however, and Vickers was instructed to continue with the original prototype – the V.630, with Darts – as mentioned above.

Production of the second prototype slowed down, but work continued on the first at Foxwarren, Vickers' experimental works near its main factories at Weybridge and Wisley. On completion, the first fuselage was transferred to Wisley for final assembly, and in June 1948 the first prototype, registered G-AHRF, was

Bearing no markings other than its registration, G-AHRF, on the rear fuselage, the prototype Vickers V.630 was rolled out of the Vickers factory at Weybridge in June 1948. The Viscount would quickly become popular with its pilots, partly owing to the unusually wide field of view from the cockpit, as seen to good advantage in this photograph taken on the day of its roll-out. Note the immaculately "dressed" paddle-props, with the blades lined up to create visual harmony. (Philip Jarrett Collection)

rolled out of the hangar in a natural metal finish and with no markings other than its registration. The following month the prototype was ready to fly, and on the damp and grey morning of July 16, Vickers' chief test pilot Joseph "Mutt" Summers, ably assisted by copilot G.R. "Jock" Bryce, took G-AHRF aloft from Wisley's grass runway for its 20min maiden flight, Summers describing the machine after landing as "the smoothest and best" he had ever flown. The aircraft was then painted in

The big day – Vickers' chief test pilot Capt Joseph "Mutt" Summers and his deputy Jock Bryce undertook the V.630's maiden flight at Vickers' airfield at Wisley, a few miles from Weybridge, on July 16, 1948. The flight comprised a 20min flight around the local area, after which Summers landed the new airliner and announced that it was a natural flyer. No major problems had arisen during the flight, Summers and Bryce reporting only a minor issue with a fuel-flow gauge. (Philip Jarrett Collection)

The Viscount's chief turboprop-powered rival was the Armstrong Whitworth AW.55 Apollo, only two of which were built. The Armstrong Siddeley Mamba engines were housed in aerodynamically efficient cowlings, but in contrast to the Dart, which also had its fair share of early development troubles, the Apollo's Mambas could not be rectified in time to secure a future for the type, and its development was discontinued in June 1952. (The Aviation Historian Archive)

The Apollo: Armstrong Whitworth's also-ran

Although Vickers led the field with the Brabazon IIB requirement, a number of other manufacturers were also asked in October 1945 to submit designs for a medium-range turboprop-powered airliner, including Blackburn (the Dart-powered B.55 and Mamba-powered B.65), Handley Page (H.P.78 with Mambas), Short Bros (S.53/SA.5) and Armstrong Whitworth. Only the latter was selected to provide a prototype, however, resulting in the handsome AW.55, originally named Achilles, to be powered by four Mambas built by the manufacturer's sister company, Armstrong Siddeley. Similar in size to the Vickers design, the Achilles was designed to accommodate 30 passengers with a range of more than 1,000 miles (1,610km) at a cruising speed no lower than 280 m.p.h. (450km/h). Two prototypes were ordered by the MoS to a revised Specification, designated 16/46. The new design was renamed Avon during 1947, but to avoid any confusion with the Rolls-Royce jet engine of the same name, it was swiftly changed again to Apollo that June.

Although the shapely Apollo showed a great deal of promise, its Mamba engines soon proved troublesome and the first prototype, with military serial VX220, did not make its maiden flight until April 10, 1949, some nine months after its Vickers rival. The prototype put in an appearance at that year's SBAC show at Farnborough with its civil registration, G-AIYN, participating in the flying display and as a static exhibit. Powerplant problems continued, however, with the Mambas able to provide only some 80 per cent of their full power owing to jetpipe temperature concerns. The Apollo was awarded a restricted CoA in October 1950, by which time BEA had already placed an order for the Viscount.

The type made one flight to Paris in March 1951, but otherwise was fully engaged in its trials programme, and the second prototype, G-AMCH/VX224, didn't fly until December 1952, bearing its military serial (it never carried its civil registration). It was too little, too late, with production plans for the Apollo having been shelved six months previously. The first prototype reverted to its military serial and both were on strength with the Aeroplane & Armament Experimental Establishment (A&AEE) at Boscombe Down by the end of 1953. After a short period of handling trials, the first prototype was returned to Armstrong Whitworth and used for metal-fatigue testing and the second went on to serve with the Empire Test Pilots School at Farnborough until the end of 1954, when it was donated to the Royal Aircraft Establishment at the same location for water-tank pressurisation tests. Ultimately the Apollo was let down by its unproven engines and, like its Vickers rival initially, was deemed too small for the purposes of its prime customer, BEA.

Vickers' somewhat restrained house colours, which British weekly *Flight* described as "light metallic blue with dark and gold markings" (although by all accounts it was in fact a standard aluminium finish) and presented to the press on September 2, 1948. Despite numerous technical setbacks and political hold-ups, the world's first turboprop-powered airliner, designed and built as such, had flown. What lay ahead now was proving that this most modern of airliners offered the key to profitability for the predicted massive expansion in post-war air travel.

Shortly after its first flight, G-AHRF had a restrained Vickers "house livery" applied, which comprised a cheat line the length of the fuselage, with the Vickers logo on the fin and nose. Between its first flight in July and its first showing to the public at the SBAC show at Farnborough in September 1948, G-AHRF completed 15hr of flying, including this sortie over Poole Harbour on the English South Coast. (The Aviation Historian Archive)

ABOVE and BELOW: Looking every inch the modern airliner, G-AHRF is presented to the press at the beginning of September 1948, during which it was demonstrated by Mutt Summers and Jock Bryce. Following its public debut at the SBAC show a few days later, the V.630 prototype made its first overseas trip, carrying four government officials to Paris, on September 20. The following month it was allocated a military serial, VX211, for further testing. (Both Philip Jarrett Collection)

The Dart turboprops of G-AHRF are run up for the gathered media during the aircraft's press debut on September 2, 1948. The Dart and the Viscount enjoyed a hugely significant symbiotic relationship, the success of one being a vital part of the success of the other. Indeed it could be argued that without the Dart, there may have been no Viscount and vice versa.
(Philip Jarrett Collection)

CHAPTER 2

Development

REGARDED AS ONE of the most important "shop windows" for British aviation and its manufacturers, the Society of British Aircraft Constructors (SBAC) show at Farnborough in Hampshire provided the perfect opportunity for Vickers to show off its thoroughly modern new airliner, and so it was that after the completion of the mandatory 15 hours of flying required to permit a type's attendance at

Following its public debut at the SBAC show at Farnborough in 1948, the Viscount was a regular visitor to the annual industry gathering over the next few years, three examples being on hand for display at the 1950 show, including the prototype, the Tay-engined VX217, seen here to the right of the massive Bristol Brabazon's tail, and the V.700 prototype, G-AMAV, seen here on the corner of the right-hand runway intersection beyond the Vickers Varsity. (The Aviation Historian Archive)

In October 1948 the V.630 prototype's civil registration was cancelled and the aircraft was allocated the military serial VX211. Although the Vickers colour scheme remained, roundels were applied on the rear fuselage and wings and fin flashes appeared on the fin. On October 29 the aircraft was flown to Rolls-Royce's airfield at Hucknall in Nottinghamshire, where the engine company's Managing Director, Ernest Hives, was taken on a flight aboard the new airliner. Hives was delighted to find that his company's Dart engines performed perfectly, providing a smooth, quiet ride. (Philip Jarrett Collection)

the show, G-AHRF arrived at the Hampshire airfield in early September 1948 in its Vickers house livery. The response of both the airlines and the general public to the elegant new airliner was extremely positive, potential operators noting the efficiency of the Darts' sleek nacelles – each containing a self-contained, easily-maintained and -changed "power egg" – and future passengers looking forward to sampling the type's trademark massive oval windows. Also of interest to its future users was the high degree of safety offered by the Viscount, which ran on low-volatility kerosene fuel and incorporated crash-proof wing tanks; innovative features at the time.

With its first public relations exercise hailed as a great success, the prototype undertook its first trip abroad a few weeks later, flying to Villacoublay, near Paris, on September 20, with the purpose of capitalising on its good showing at Farnborough and generating more interest from prospective customers. No orders were forthcoming at this point, however, and G-AHRF returned to the UK to continue its trials programme under its military serial, VX211.

As the prototype was put through its paces during the summer of 1948, good news arrived from Rolls-Royce, which had developed and uprated the Dart to deliver 40 per cent more power than the variant fitted to G-AHRF, opening the door to an improved airframe with larger wings and a longer fuselage, which, with a high-density seating configuration, could accommodate up to 53 passengers, much more in line with BEA's requirements and a meaningful riposte to the airline's concerns that the type was too small to be economical.

As mentioned, George Edwards had already explored a slightly larger version back in mid-1947 and the uprated R.Da 3 (Mk 504) Dart made a larger, more economical Viscount a very real proposition. Accordingly, the 1947 plans were dusted off and the new "stretched" version was designated V.700. After a little financial legerdemain by Vickers and the men from the ministry, the MoS ordered a V.700 prototype in February 1949 to Specification 21/49, the manufacturer using some of the components of the abandoned private-venture third prototype at Foxwarren as the basis of the revised design. However, with Valiant bomber work taking priority (and most of the floorspace) at Foxwarren, the new Viscount

(The Aviation Historian Archive)

ABOVE and BELOW: While undertaking its rigorous testing programme as VX211, the V.630 was also loaned back to Vickers for various demonstrations during 1949, including several for BEA and BOAC and the International Civil Aviation Organisation. There were also regular press demonstrations during which the prototype would be flown with various propellers feathered (including both on the same side) to show the type's wide safety margin.

(Philip Jarrett Collection)

fuselage had to be transported to the Vickers-Armstrongs (Supermarine) factory at South Marston; the wings were to be built at Itchen, near Southampton.

In the meantime the flying trials of G-AHRF/VX211 continued, and the press was given its first opportunity to appraise the new type in depth in December 1948, when journalists were invited on a flight aboard the aircraft with George Edwards. When asked if he was satisfied that all the "bugs" had been ironed out, Edwards characteristically replied: "That's what's worrying us – we can't find any!"

Testing continued into 1949 and after the accrual of 290 flying hours over the course of 160 flights, the prototype was awarded a Certificate of Airworthiness (CoA) on September 15 that year. It was initially a restricted CoA as cold-weather

ABOVE and BELOW: In August 1949 the V.630 was returned to Vickers and re-allocated its civil registration, G-AHRF. The legend "British European Airways" was applied in small letters along the fuselage above the windows and a Union flag replaced the military flash on either side of the fin. The aircraft continued its extensive testing and demonstration work, the latter including flights for representatives of numerous airlines including Air-India, American Overseas Airlines, Panair do Brasil and Pan American World Airways among others. (Philip Jarrett Collection)

and tropical trials, scheduled for the following year, had yet to be completed. The prototype's next showing was its second visit to the SBAC show at Farnborough, which in 1949 boasted an impressive collection of state-of-the-art airliners, including four British types powered by turboprop engines – the Viscount, Handley Page Hermes 5, Armstrong Whitworth Apollo (see panel on page 16) and Handley Page Marathon 2 – so it was no surprise that some 15 major airlines from around the world sent representatives to investigate the potential of these new cutting-edge aircraft. Of the four turboprops, however, only the Viscount would be put into production.

The beginning of 1950 saw the prototype despatched to Shannon on the west coast of Ireland for trials of the de-icing system, which worked perfectly, and by March it had been painted in an elegant new BEA colour scheme in preparation for a European sales tour in association with the airline (which, it is worth remembering, had yet to place an official order for the Viscount). Not only would the tour offer invaluable publicity for the new type, it would also serve to put the airliner through

By March 1950 G-AHRF had been painted in a full BEA livery, and on the 20th of that month it departed on an eight-city European capital tour. In June the same year G-AHRF set off for tropical trials in Khartoum, Sudan, accompanied by officials from Vickers, BEA, Rolls-Royce and the Aeroplane & Armament Experimental Establishment, all keen to see how the new turboprop would behave in "hot and high" conditions. The tour also included visits to Kenya, Egypt, Libya, Malta and France. (The Aviation Historian Archive)

its paces under operational conditions, which BEA was keen to investigate.

Leaving Northolt on March 20, 1950, with BEA Captain W.J. Wakelin in command, G-AHRF visited Amsterdam, Brussels, Zürich, Rome and Paris over the following three weeks, returning back to the UK for the Easter Bank Holiday, before setting off again on April 11 for Copenhagen, Stockholm, Oslo and another visit to Amsterdam. By the time it made its final return home on April 28, G-AHRF had covered some 4,400 miles (7,080km) during 70 flights and accrued a total of 61 flying hours. The trip also allowed some new techniques to be tested, including two-engined descents from altitude in order to conserve fuel, which proved entirely practicable, although it was never adopted for operational airline service. As *Flight* reported at the time: "At two destinations the aircraft had to stand off because of bad weather and, again, seemed very happy when doing so on only two engines".

In early June 1950 G-AHRF was off again, this time to conduct tropical trials at Khartoum in Sudan and Nairobi in Kenya, the latter being more than 5,000ft (1,525m) above sea level. The results were again excellent, and proved that the new airliner could operate successfully in "hot and high" conditions with or without the use of a supplemental water/methanol injection boost system. With the trials completed, the aircraft returned to the UK on July 10.

A little more than two weeks later the Viscount was rewarded for completing

During the summer of 1950 G-AHRF was loaned from Vickers to BEA in order to undertake route-proving trials for the airline. July 29 saw the first scheduled turboprop commercial flight when the aircraft completed the 70min flight from London's Northolt airport to Le Bourget in Paris on service BE392X2. Passengers on the service received a letter from BEA's Chief Executive Peter Masefield, who explained the historic significance of the flight and gave a brief description of the aircraft and the Dart engines that powered it. The letter concluded with "In this preview of the future, BEA is delighted to have you as one of its passengers". (Philip Jarrett Collection)

Seen here with the mighty Bristol Brabazon in the background at the 1950 SBAC show, the V.700 prototype, G-AMAV, provided a spirited display in the hands of Jock Bryce, whose routine included dynamic flying passes with three of the four propellers feathered. The aircraft was very lightly loaded, but it was still quite a feat of airmanship and an excellent demonstration of the Dart engine's power. (The Aviation Historian Archive)

its exhausting trials programme with the issue of its full CoA, thus clearing the way for one of its most important acid-tests – its introduction into scheduled service with fare-paying passengers. History was made on Saturday, July 29, 1950, when G-AHRF took off from Northolt for Paris-Le Bourget on the world's first scheduled turboprop air service. The aircraft plied the London—Paris route for BEA for the next two weeks, carrying more than 1,500 passengers and prompting the airline to sign a contract in early August for 20 examples of the larger 700-series, which had yet to fly. The V.630 prototype was also used for a week-long series of daily flights to Edinburgh for BEA in mid-August, after which it was returned to Vickers to continue its test programme.

In the meantime work had gathered pace on the third airframe, which was now the V.700 prototype, the wingspan of which was some 5ft (1·5m) greater than that of the V.630 and the fuselage of which was 7ft 4in (2·2m) longer than its predecessor. By April 1950 the various completed parts of the airframe had been transported to the Vickers factory at Weybridge for final assembly, and on August 28 the V.700 prototype, registered G-AMAV and painted in BEA colours, made its first flight in the hands of Jock Bryce, who reported no problems on landing at nearby Wisley. Powered by four Dart 504s G-AMAV was quickly put through a series of flights to gain the flying hours required to appear at the SBAC show, which opened a mere eight days later, and where Jock Bryce flew a dazzling display, throwing the Viscount around as though it was a nimble fighter, with various combinations of engines shut down to demonstrate the type's safety. It came as something of a relief to Vickers when BEA placed an order for 20 V.701s in August 1950 (and another six shortly afterwards, plus another in 1956), although sales remained slow enough for Vickers to remain jittery until Air France placed an order for 12 V.708s in November 1951, Aer Lingus following on its heels with an order for four V.707s, each operator being given its own 700-series designation.

The prototype V.700 sailed through its trials programme, tropical trials being

The V.700 prototype was used extensively for trials and promotional tours, including a three-month stint in Africa in 1955, for which it was fitted with Dart 510 engines and square-tipped propellers, both starboard examples of which are seen feathered in this photograph of the aircraft in the Vickers colour scheme it wore during 1955–56. After more trials it was put into storage at Wisley in the spring of 1958 and the registration G-AMAV was cancelled in 1960; the fuselage was broken up the following year. (The Aviation Historian Archive)

undertaken in South Africa during October–November 1951, which also provided an excellent opportunity to promote the type's reliability and passenger-friendliness to a valuable prospective market. With icing trials completed in early 1952 the type was awarded its CoA that June, the same month that G-AMAV visited India and Pakistan on a promotional tour and Trans-Australia Airlines ordered six V.720s with extra fuel tankage.

By the time the first production V.701 for BEA, G-ALWE, was ready to make its maiden flight on August 20, 1952, Vickers had secured orders for 48 aircraft from four airlines, and was negotiating with various airlines from around the world for 50 more. Arguably one of the most important early orders, however, came from Trans-Canada Air Lines (TCAL) in November 1952, when the company became the first North American operator to select the Viscount, ordering 15 examples modified to TCAL's bespoke requirements and designated V.724. The Canadian operator's faith in the new turboprop was infectious, and its order would lead to the type's selection by the USA's Capital Airlines in 1954, which signified a major breakthrough for Vickers and the Viscount in the lucrative American market. With the order book swelling and production examples starting to come off the line, the Viscount was finally ready to begin its long and illustrious service career.

A contemporary Vickers-Armstrongs brochure for the Viscount 700, in which part of the introduction reads: "From the airline operator's point of view the idea aircraft combines a high payload with economical cruising and the maximum safety factor. At the same time, in order to attract travellers who might be inclined to use other means of travel, the airliner must show a considerable saving in time. This has been achieved in the production Viscount 700". (Philip Jarrett Collection)

Giving a fine view of the Viscount's distinctive straight-taper wing and flap arrangement, the first production V.701, G-ALWE makes a pass at the 1952 SBAC show at Farnborough in the hands of future Concorde test pilot Brian Trubshaw. Fitted with Dart 505s, G-ALWE was delivered to BEA in January 1953 in a 40-seat first-class configuration with two rows of two seats separated by the aisle, but it was swiftly reconfigured with a 47-seat all-tourist class layout before it entered service. (Philip Jarrett Collection)

Named *RMA Discovery*, G-ALWE operated the inaugural BEA Viscount services to a number of European cities including Cologne (on January 22, 1953), Zürich (March 19, 1953), Rome, Athens and Istanbul (all on April 19, 1953). Sadly, on March 14, 1957, the aircraft suffered a structural failure in the flap system and crashed into a house near Manchester Airport, killing 15 passengers and five crew, along with two people on the ground. (Philip Jarrett Collection)

The Tay Viscount

(The Aviation Historian Archive)

One of the more interesting variations on the Viscount was the Ministry of Supply's decision in 1948 to complete the second prototype as an experimental engine testbed fitted with a pair of Rolls-Royce centrifugal-flow Tay turbojets of 6,250lb-thrust each. Work started on converting the second prototype to jet power at Foxwarren but was completed at Wisley, by which time it had been given a military serial, VX217, and a new Vickers designation, V.663. On March 15, 1950, Jock Bryce took the Tay Viscount aloft for the first time. Essentially the same as the V.630 in terms of dimensions and layout, VX217 differed only in having new engine pods, which incorporated a revised undercarriage design. Along with its considerably quieter Dart-powered sister, VX217 participated in the 1950 SBAC show – its only public appearance – that September, impressing the crowds with its short take-off run and spritely performance.

In October 1952 the Tay Viscount was leased to Boulton Paul at Defford for electronic flying-control systems research and was also used by the Decca Navigator Co for various trials. While being operated by Boulton Paul at its base at Seighford in 1958, VX217 was written off after a hydraulic fire burnt through the mainspar, and was scrapped in 1960 having accrued a relatively meagre 110hr 15min of flying time.

(Philip Jarrett Collection)

The unique second prototype Viscount airframe, originally intended to be fitted with Armstrong Siddeley Mamba turboprops, was allocated military serial VX217 and fitted with a pair of Rolls-Royce Tay turbojets instead and given the designation V.663. It first flew in March 1950 and made its only public appearance at that year's SBAC show at Farnborough. Aside from the alternative powerplants, and associated wing and undercarriage alterations, the airframe was essentially the same as the V.630 prototype, G-AHRF. The aircraft remained in a bare-metal finish with roundels and fin flashes throughout its career, which ended after a hydraulic failure occurred in a wheel bay and set the aircraft on fire while on the ground at Seighford on December 31, 1958.

When an air race from London to Christchurch, New Zealand, was announced in 1953, BEA, Vickers and Rolls-Royce all leapt at the chance to promote the Viscount and its Dart engines in a short- to medium-haul environment to which it would be eminently suited. The 700-series prototype, G-AMAV, was duly lent from the Ministry of Supply and given race number "23" for the race, which began on October 8, 1953. Reportedly, John Profumo, then a junior aviation minister, served as chef and steward aboard the aircraft during its three-day journey to Christchurch. (Philip Jarrett Collection)

Turboprop down under: the London – New Zealand Air Race, 1953

In 1948 the largest city on the South Island of New Zealand, Christchurch, celebrated the centenary of its founding. The idea of an air race from the UK to New Zealand was mooted, generating a great deal of interest from prospective participants. For various reasons nothing came of the plan until 1953, by which time the number of interested parties had diminished considerably; BEA nevertheless saw an invaluable opportunity to promote its new turboprop in a region for which it would be eminently suited and quickly threw its hat into the ring. Viscount G-AMNZ, aptly named *James Cook*, was earmarked to take part, but in the event could not be released from its busy schedule. The airline prevailed on the MoS to loan the prototype V.700 in its place, and G-AMAV was duly painted in BEA colours, named *RMA Endeavour* and given the racing number "23". It was also modified to carry extra fuel tanks in the cabin, the Viscount having been designed for medium-haul rather than long-haul routes.

On October 8, 1953, the eight aircraft participating in the race, including three RAF and two RAAF English Electric Canberras, an RNZAF Handley Page Hastings and a KLM Douglas DC-6A, departed Heathrow airport. Taking off 10min after the Dutch DC-6A, G-AMAV landed 10hr 10min later at Bahrain, having averaged some 310 m.p.h. (500km/h). After refuelling in 14min, the Viscount was off again, bound for Negombo in Ceylon (now Sri Lanka), where it once again performed a whistle-stop refuelling before heading out for tiny West Island, one of the Cocos (Keeling) Islands in the Indian Ocean. After a 22min refuelling stop, G-AMAV took off from the remote island strip to complete the longest leg of the course, which covered 3,500 miles (5,630km) to Melbourne in Australia, which it reached in 10hr 15min having achieved a remarkable average speed of 350 m.p.h. (563km/h) at 35,000ft (10,670m). Although the Viscount arrived some nine hours before the DC-6A – the only remaining aircraft in the handicap section (the Hastings having retired in the Cocos Islands) – it was the Dutch aircraft that took the honours owing to the handicapping system. Nevertheless, the race generated valuable publicity for the turboprop and G-AMAV returned to the UK at a somewhat more leisurely pace via several points in Australia, Singapore, India, Cyprus and Italy, giving demonstrations to numerous airlines and operators along the way.

CHAPTER 3

Into Service

BY THE BEGINNING of 1954 the Viscount order book was swelling at a satisfying rate, with orders arriving from British airline Hunting-Clan, BOAC associate British West Indian Airways and, importantly, the first Middle Eastern Viscount operator in the form of Iraqi Airways, which ordered three V.735s in the summer of 1953. With Trans-Canada having ordered the type in late 1952, it was hoped that short- and medium-haul operators below the 49th Parallel would sit up and take notice, and Vickers-Armstrongs began an aggressive marketing campaign to attract American domestic airlines. The first significant interest shown by an American company, however, was the result of a fact-finding mission sent to the UK by J.H. Carmichael, President of Washington DC-based regional operator Capital Airlines. Not convinced by the available alternative homegrown options, including the

Trans Canada Air Lines first Viscount V.724, CF-TGI (c/n 40), has its Darts run up before its delivery to the airline in Winnipeg in December 1954. The following March the aircraft was demonstrated to representatives of American operators and the press at Idlewild airport in New York, in the hope that it might open up the USA as an extremely lucrative market for the new turboprop, despite America's complete dominance of the airliner market at the time. (Philip Jarrett Collection)

When British West Indian Airways (BWIA), one of BOAC's Associated Companies, ordered its first three Viscount V.702s in June 1953, the 700-series prototype, G-AMAV, was painted in the airline's colours (as seen here) and displayed at the SBAC show at Farnborough in September 1954, by which time a fourth example had been ordered. All four of BWIA's Viscounts were fitted with the latest radar equipment, enabling them to see up to 150 miles (240km) ahead and thus avoid bad weather. The airline operated Viscount services around the Caribbean and up to New York, and was so impressed with the aircraft that it ordered four more, designated V.772s, which arrived in late 1957 and early 1958. (The Aviation Historian Archive)

In October 1955 Iraqi Airways ordered three Viscounts, designated V.735s, becoming one of the first operators in the Middle East to modernise its fleet. The third V.735, YI-ACM (c/n 69), seen here beside the distinctive BOAC hangar at Heathrow in September 1956, was named *Ibn Battouta* in honour of the medieval Muslim traveller and scholar, and was delivered to Baghdad in December 1955. The aircraft continued to serve with Iraqi Airways until the mid-1970s, and it was sold in 1978 to Alidair and re-registered as G-BFYZ. It was ultimately written off in a landing accident on October 25, 1979. Happily, there were no injuries. (Mike Hooks)

Following TCAL's order in 1952, another vitally important sale for the Viscount came in the summer of 1954, when the President of Capital Airlines, J.H. Carmichael (seen here on the right, talking to George Edwards beside a Viscount), announced a major order for the type, including three V.744s and 60 V.745Ds. Carmichael and Capital were taking a big risk on the new airliner, and drew brickbats from the American press for not selecting a homegrown product. In terms of profitability, the Viscount more than repaid such a leap of faith. (Philip Jarrett Collection)

piston-engined Convair 240/340 series, Carmichael was keen to explore the potential of a turboprop, which offered the flexibility required to make his network of short regional flights and longer inter-city routes profitable. Carmichael's task force liked what it saw, and in June 1954 Capital announced an initial order for three V.744s with a 48-seat configuration and powered by four Dart 506s, these first three actually being taken from BEA's order, with the British airline's permission, to enable Capital to begin Viscount services at the earliest possible opportunity. It is almost impossible to overstate the importance of Capital's commitment to a type designed and built outside the USA, at that time the undisputed world leader in commercial aircraft production. Indeed, it was with some bravery that Capital faced brutal opposition from various quarters at home, including American aircraft manufacturers and political commentators. Vickers was appreciative of Capital's leap of faith and bent over backwards to accommodate the airline's needs in terms of service and training. As a result, by the end of 1954, some six months before the delivery of its first example, Capital had ordered another 60 Viscounts, these to be V.745s with modifications including integral airstairs, with another 15 ordered in July 1956, although these were never delivered to the airline.

A classic contemporary advertisement extolling the virtues of the Viscount in service with Trans Canada Air Lines (TCAL), which had placed an extremely significant order for 15 V.724s in November 1952. George Edwards had personally overseen the presentation of the aircraft to TCAL's executives, understanding that a foot-hold in the North American market would be vital if the Viscount was to become a major player on the world stage. (David H. Stringer Collection)

RIGHT: Having placed its order for a total of 63 Viscounts, Capital Airlines' marketing department went into overdrive, this contemporary magazine advertisement emphasising the advantages of the new airliner to prospective customers who may not have flown before: "You'll be flying the world's most modern airliner, powered by four Rolls-Royce turboprop engines and proved by more than a billion passenger miles. The quiet elegance of the Viscount is preferred by experienced travellers everywhere . . ." (David H. Stringer Collection)

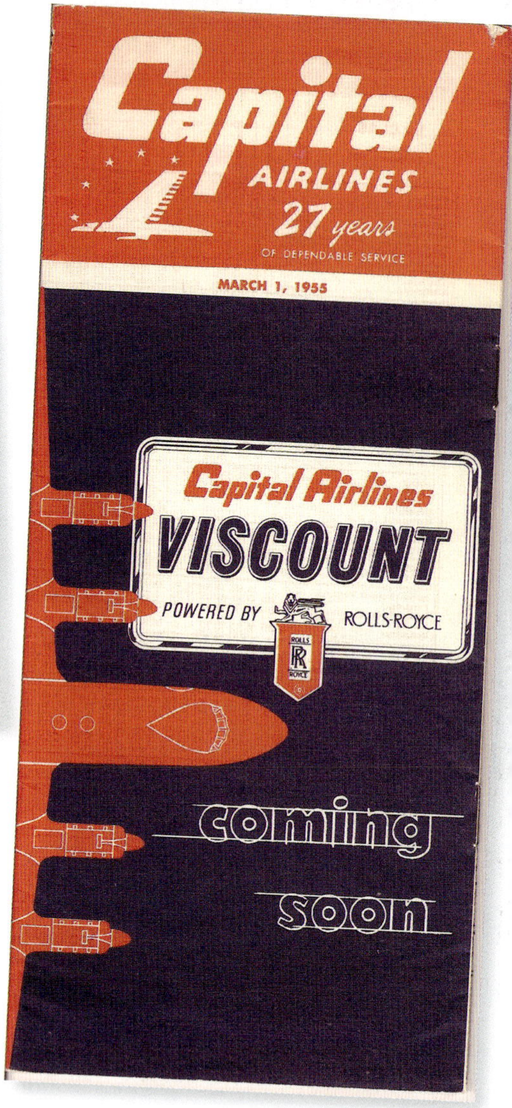

RIGHT: A March 1955 Capital Airlines timetable heralding the Viscount's arrival into service that July. By December the same year Capital was announcing that it was selling more Viscount seats than on any other aircraft then being used in America, and that the airline's load factors had increased by some 80 per cent since the Viscount had entered service – the advertising had clearly worked. (David H. Stringer Collection)

An important European order came in 1951, when Air France ordered six V.708s, including F-BGNR (c/n 35), which was built at Hurn and made its first flight on May 30, 1954. Some airlines' liveries suited the Viscount's shapely lines, none more so than Air France's handsome colour scheme of the 1950s, incorporating a bare-metal finish on the undersides, a white cabin roof and the operator's distinctive winged sea-horse, which is just visible on the fin in this photograph taken in June 1959. (Mike Hooks)

Leading the line on the Weybridge production line in 1952 is second production V.701 G-ALWF (c/n 5), which has already had its BEA Discovery-Class name *RMA Sir John Franklin* applied, in honour of the British Royal Navy officer and Arctic explorer. The same year, a decision was taken to set up another production line at Hurn using Hangars 106 and 107, the first Viscount from the new line flying in December 1953. (Philip Jarrett Collection)

In June 1955 the first V.744 was delivered to Capital at Washington DC, the airline's marketing machine going into overdrive to promote its fleet of state-of-the-art turboprops. The USA's first scheduled turboprop service was inaugurated on July 26, 1955, with a first-class Capital Viscount round trip between Washington DC and Chicago. Vickers had managed to jam a foot in the door of the vital American market, and orders from Continental and Northeast Airlines quickly followed suit.

Meanwhile, production was gathering pace at Vickers' Weybridge factory, where the first 24 700-series Viscounts – 18 for BEA and six for Air France – were completed. With the factory also engaged in production of the Valiant bomber and a rapidly swelling Viscount order book, it was decided to establish a new production line for the turboprop at Hurn, near Bournemouth on the British South Coast. The first Hurn-built Viscount, G-AMOO for BEA, made its maiden flight from the factory airfield on December 1, 1953. Demand for the Viscount grew to such an extent, however, that a production line had to be re-opened at Weybridge, a decision that would pay dividends later with the introduction of the improved 800-series from 1956. Some 279 of the total of 444 Viscounts built came off the Hurn production line. To keep up with demand, the production of Viscount wings was subcontracted to Saunders-Roe on the Isle of Wight, Vickers proudly announcing

The first of five V.748Ds ordered by Central African Airways (CAA) in July 1954, VP-YNA (c/n 98) is seen here during an aerial photography sortie before its delivery to Salisbury in Rhodesia in April 1956. The airline had been established in 1946 by the governments of Northern Rhodesia, Southern Rhodesia and Nyasaland, and was reconstituted when the three nations became the new British Commonwealth nations of Zambia, Rhodesia and Malawi respectively. The airline continued to operate as CAA until the end of 1966, after Rhodesia had unilaterally declared its independence, which led to the Viscounts being redistributed to Air Malawi and Air Rhodesia, VP-YNA going to the former. (The Aviation Historian Archive)

that, when aggregated, its Viscount production line was more than a mile long. By 1957 the company was producing a remarkable ten Viscounts per month, a record for any British airliner before or since.

With the breakthrough in North American sales, thanks to the Trans-Canada and Capital orders, the Viscount became the "must-have" item for numerous airlines all over the world, orders flooding in from Central African Airways, Hong Kong Airways, LAV of Venezuela and various others. By the end of 1956 the 200th Viscount order had been received, production of the 700-series stretching to a total of 288 aircraft, comprising 138 700s and 150 700Ds, the last example, a Misrair V.739, making its maiden flight in March 1960.

Enter the Viscount 800

Back in 1952, before the 700-series had entered service, Vickers was already looking to develop a stretched version of its new airliner, which would also offer superior operating economics. Having had initial doubts about the type's size, and therefore its profitability, from the outset, BEA was obviously also keen to explore the possibility of a larger version. The proposed V.801 for BEA was to have its fuselage lengthened by a generous 13ft 3in (4m) and be powered by four 1,690 s.h.p. R.Da 5 Darts, to accommodate 86 tourist-class seats in a high-density layout. After some extensive arithmetic by Vickers and BEA, however, it was ascertained that for various reasons the V.801 would in fact offer inferior performance to the 700-series, mainly owing to the 801's greater weight, which would see its cruising speed fall below 300 m.p.h. (485km/h). Although BEA had committed

Having made its first flight in August 1957, Viscount V.803 PH-VID (c/n 175), named *Otto Lilienthal* after the German aeronautical pioneer, appeared at that year's SBAC show at Farnborough in its gleaming new KLM colours. The Dutch airline had not acquired 700-series Viscounts, being a faithful customer of American manufacturer Convair, but the superior economics of the British airliner in terms of capacity and ease of operation were undeniable, and KLM became the lead export customer for the 800-series. (The Aviation Historian Archive)

to purchasing 12 V.801s in late 1952, the order was quietly set aside, although the airline was still interested in a stretched variant, leading Vickers to come up with an alternative.

The new variant, referred to initially by BEA as the "Viscount Major", introduced a much more modest stretch of 3ft 10in (1·2m), but with an ingenious method of extending the passenger cabin. This entailed moving the rear pressure bulkhead aft by 5ft 5in (1·7m), thereby creating some 9ft 3in (2·8m) of extra space, which could be filled with additional rows of seats. A number of other modifications were also devised, including the replacement of the often-unwieldy oval fuselage doors (front and rear) with more orthodox rectangular doors which lay flat against the fuselage when open (and which quickly became a reliable method of telling an 800-series from a 700-series). Moveable cabin bulkheads were also incorporated which allowed a modular approach in terms of compartmentalising the cabin into freight and passenger areas, giving the type a "QC" – quick change – capability. The strengthened wing spars incorporated into Capital's V.745/745Ds were also fitted to 800-series Viscounts as standard. Importantly, the 1,740 s.h.p. R.Da 6 Dart (510) was available by this time, which, with the reduced stretch and resultant lower weight-gain, pushed the new variant's cruising speed up to around 325 m.p.h. (523km/h). The new variant was much more the ticket as far as BEA was concerned, the airline re-allocating its initial order for 12 V.801s in favour of the new V.802, as it was designated, in April 1954, and ordering another 12 by the end of 1955. Other airlines were quick to show interest in the new variant, Dutch airline KLM becoming its first export customer when it ordered nine V.803s in June 1955 for use on the airline's busier European and Middle Eastern services. The Dutch order was a significant one, KLM having previously been a staunch Convair customer.

There was no prototype of the 800-series, the first example becoming BEA's

Viscount V.804 G-AOXU (c/n 248) peels away from the camera aircraft during a photographic sortie shortly before its delivery to Airwork subsidiary Transair in September 1957. Transair's work consisted mainly of trooping flights and its Viscounts were unusual in having 58 rearward-facing seats and a "mother's room", incorporating four cots, in the rear. In May 1958 this aircraft earned the distinction of being the first commercial airliner to land at the newly opened Gatwick Airport, when it set down at the end of a trooping flight from Gibraltar. (The Aviation Historian Archive)

flagship V.802, G-AOJA, named *Sir Samuel White Baker*, which made its maiden flight on July 27, 1956, two months after which it was exhibited at the 1956 SBAC show at Farnborough. Sadly it was destroyed during a landing accident at Belfast (Nutts Corner) in October 1957, having flown a mere 1,472 hours.

Viscount V.802 services were inaugurated by BEA on the London—Paris route in February 1957, the airline utilising a 57-seat all-tourist configuration, which suited BEA's short high-density routes. Other airlines with similar sector lengths quickly showed an interest, orders coming in from British charter airlines Transair and Eagle Aviation.

With the implementation of the stretch programme and the successful entry of the 800-series into service, the Viscount had proven itself as a supremely desirable and economical airliner with a built-in flexibility for future development; indeed, there was more to come from the Viscount yet.

ABOVE and BELOW: Named *RMA Sir Samuel White Baker* in honour of the British 19th Century explorer, Weybridge-built Viscount V.802 G-AOJA (c/n 150) made its first flight on July 27, 1956, and made an appearance at that year's SBAC show at Farnborough, where it is seen above on the "piano keys". Tragically its career was cut short on October 23, 1957, when it crashed in fog on approach to Nutts Corner (Belfast). The subsequent investigation revealed that the aircraft's undercarriage was fully retracted when it hit the ground, but also ascertained that pilot error was not to blame – it concluded that the accident, in which the five crew and two passengers were killed, "must remain a wholly unexplained calamity".
(Above: Mike Stroud via The Aviation Historian Archive. Below: The Aviation Historian Archive)

When the Convair 240 was introduced into airline service in 1948, its rate of climb was much praised and it was very much seen as an ideal replacement for the dependable but ageing DC-3. The type formed the blueprint for a number of developments, Convair very much subscribing to the "evolution, not revolution" ethos. (The Aviation Historian Archive)

The competition: Convair and Martin

Vickers was not the only company to foresee the demand for a post-war airliner, and it was the Americans that offered the first serious contender in the competition to develop what came to be seen as the holy grail for post-war commercial operators — a DC-3 replacement. San Diego-based Convair, a conglomeration of Consolidated and Vultee, was quick off the mark with its Model 110, an unpressurised twin-piston-engined low-wing all-metal monoplane, which first flew in July 1946. Realising that airlines would require a pressurised aircraft, Convair developed the Model 110 into the CV-240, a 40-seat airliner with a tricycle undercarriage and powered by a pair of Pratt & Whitney R-2800 Double Wasp radial piston engines. The CV-240 made its maiden flight on March 16, 1947, more than a year before the turboprop-powered Viscount, and was soon gaining orders from airlines including American Airlines, Western Air Lines, Trans-Australia Airlines and KLM, the last two later becoming important Viscount customers.

Similar in configuration and using the same powerplant as the CV-240 was the unpressurised Martin 2-0-2, which first flew in November 1946, and which entered service in the summer of 1947, having been purchased by Northwest Airlines and TWA in the USA and LAN Chile and LAV in South America. Soon after the 2-0-2 and CV-240 had entered service, both companies realised that their respective types warranted further development. Martin offered the pressurised 4-0-4, slightly larger and with structural improvements (although still piston-powered), the prototype making its maiden flight in October 1950. The type entered service in 1951 with Eastern Airlines. A total of 103 4-0-4s was built.

Convair cleaned up and improved the CV-240, resulting in the CV-340, with a longer fuselage and longer-span wings, and which first flew in October 1951. Sales of the piston-powered CV-340 were healthy, with important customers including United Airlines in the USA and KLM in Europe. However, the "aspirated cooling" system of the Convairliner, as it was known, created high levels of noise in the passenger cabin, a problem which was thrown into even sharper focus when compared to the subtle whistle of the turboprops of its chief rival, the elegant Viscount. As a result Convair set to work on improving the 340's noise levels, the modified CV-440 Metropolitan (first flight October 6, 1955) introducing a baffle-box exhaust system which offered better cabin noise characteristics. Convair persisted in sticking with piston power for the 440, but also began developing turboprop versions, including the Napier Eland-powered CV-540 and the CV-580, powered by four Allison 501s, both of which variants were conversions of piston-engined 340s and 440s. Darts were also ultimately fitted to the Convairliner, providing the motive power for the CV-600 and CV-640 models.

More competition: the Lockheed Electra

A more direct competitor to the Viscount was Lockheed's Model 188 Electra, designed from the outset as a modern turboprop capable of stealing market share from the wildly successful British interloper. Capital Airlines' order for 60 Viscounts in 1954 caused something of an earthquake in the American airline industry, which was forced to realise that the dawn of the fledgling jet age had come. Interestingly, Capital had approached Lockheed before placing its Viscount order, with a view to exploring the development of a turboprop short/medium-haul airliner, the American manufacturer having had experience with turboprop power in the design of its L-1249 Super Constellation and C-130 Hercules military transport. Although Lockheed was certainly willing to undertake such a project, the company received little interest in it from any other American carriers, forcing Capital to place its historic Viscount order.

American Airlines had also approached Lockheed about a similar turboprop short-haul airliner, which met with similar indifference and on which design-study work was also stopped. Undaunted, American updated its specification and resubmitted it to Lockheed, this time calling for a four-engined 75-seater with a range of more than 2,000 miles (3,215km). If the range could be pushed to 2,500 miles (4,020km) Eastern Air Lines would also be interested, and after Lockheed concluded that it was indeed possible, American and Eastern committed to 35 and 40 examples respectively. Having experience of the Allison 501 already, Lockheed chose to fit the new type, designated Model 188, with the American turboprop, completing the prototype in a mere 26 months, by which time the company had secured 129 firm orders from six major airlines in the USA and three foreign carriers.

Eight weeks ahead of schedule, the prototype Model 188 Electra, as the type had been named, made its first flight from the Lockheed factory at Palmdale, California, on December 6, 1957, the type receiving its FAA Type Certificate in August 1958 on completion of a

The prototype Lockheed L-188 Electra, N1881, made its first flight on December 6, 1957. The Allison 501 turboprop-powered Electra was some 104ft 6in (32m) long, the stretched Viscount 800-series reaching only 85ft (26m), although the American airliner's 99ft (30m) wingspan was comparable to that of the Viscount at 93ft 8½in (28·5m).
(The Aviation Historian Archive)

Although it was late to the party, the Electra looked set to offer some serious opposition to the Viscount, but a number of crashes during 1959–60 undermined public confidence in the type and its sales fell far short of the Viscount's.
(The Aviation Historian Archive)

remarkably trouble-free trials programme. Two months later Eastern Air Lines accepted the first of seven Electras delivered to the airline that year, with American Airlines receiving four by the end of 1958. Larger than the Viscount, the Electra could accommodate 66–80 passengers in a standard layout, or up to 98 in a high-density configuration, the type offering excellent economics for American short and medium-haul operators. While the Electra looked set to give the Viscount a bruising run for its money, a number of extenuating circumstances blighted the new airliner. A pilot's strike at the end of 1958 delayed the Electra entering service at a time when it needed to capitalise on its advantages over the Viscount, and a nationwide economic slowdown in the USA at the same time inevitably slowed sales. Finally entering service with Eastern and American in January 1959, the type garnered sales from National Airlines, Western Air Lines, Braniff, Trans-Australia Airlines, Northwest Airlines, KLM, Qantas and TEAL among others. The future looked rosy for the Electra. However, three crashes (one American, one Braniff and one Northwest) between February 1959 and March 1960 seriously undermined public confidence in the aircraft, the cause later being established as a problem with the engine mountings, which were prone to vibration which led to wing flexing and ultimately failure of the wing at the root. At its own expense, Lockheed undertook a comprehensive remedial programme, but the damage had been done – Electra sales never fully recovered and only 170 were built.

CHAPTER 4

Anatomy

ON ITS INTRODUCTION into service in 1953 the Viscount was the epitome of the modern short/medium-haul airliner, with its state-of-the-art turboprop engines, luxurious interior and distinctive large oval windows, which afforded spectacular views of the world passing by below. Aside from its innovative powerplants, however, the type was of essentially orthodox construction, with a stressed-skin semi-monocoque fuselage of circular cross-section and low-set flush-riveted wings approximately midway along the length of the fuselage. Indeed, *Flight* described

While the Viscount represented the cutting-edge of airliner technology when it was introduced in the late 1940s, its construction was essentially similar to that of its predecessor, the Viking, although the lessons learned during the latter's development were incorporated in the new airliner, a 700-series of which is seen here undergoing maintenance. (Philip Jarrett Collection)

the type's design as "advanced but not rashly adventurous". The differences between the early 700-series and later 800-series in terms of general construction were minimal and the description here takes a look at a standard production 700-series Viscount.

Fuselage

The Viscount's aluminium skin was riveted to a frame made up of circular rings, soundproofing being incorporated into the skinning, which was then covered by the internal cabin wall. As the aircraft was pressurised, Vickers went to great lengths to ensure that the resulting stresses were evenly distributed. With a cabin pressure differential of up to 6·5lb/in^2, the highest of any airliner at that time, the Viscount's various apertures — windows and doors etc — were of an elliptical shape, which meant that an approximately equal stress was sustained on the apertures' boundaries. This was partly the reason for the Viscount's generously-proportioned windows, which offered such splendid views for the passenger. The British Air Registration Board had suggested that the minimum dimensions for airliner emergency exits should be 26in (66cm) high by 19in (48cm) wide, which Vickers used as a blueprint for the new airliner's windows. A pneumatic system

The port rearmost pair of seats in a Hunting-Clan Viscount V.732 (note the company's crest on the bulkhead). The seats were fully adjustable and in Hunting-Clan's case, of light-coloured material. Note also the type's distinctive large oval windows, the view from which in this position, aft of the wing, would have been spectacular.
(Steven Greensted Collection)

A typical Hunting-Clan 53-seat configuration as fitted to its V.732s, comprising nine rows of five abreast and rows of four and two abreast making up the remaining eight. The Viscount's passenger cabin was designed to offer a high degree of flexibility in terms of layout and Vickers worked closely with individual airlines to devise the most suitable configuration for each.
(Steven Greensted Collection)

was used to inflate the seals around the doors in the pressure cabin and thus keep them airtight.

Early 700-series Viscounts were fitted with an external ventral intake scoop which fed the air-conditioning system, although this was replaced with an aerodynamically cleaner flush intake on later production variants. The cockpit offered a state-of-the-art "office" for its pilots, with the most modern instrumentation laid out in an organised fashion which provided the pilots with everything they needed to

BEA Viscount V.701 G-AMOC (c/n 13), named *RMA Sir Richard Chancellor* in honour of the British 16th-Century explorer, was photographed for weekly magazine *Flight* over Shoreham-by-Sea on the English South Coast in 1954. The excrescence on the underside of the fuselage is the ventral air scoop for the air-conditioning system, which was subsequently replaced with a flush intake during ongoing production.
(The Aviation Historian Archive)

The "office" of a BEA Viscount V.802, the new variant being fitted with the Decca Flight Log system, which incorporated a moving-map display, seen here beneath the central windshield panel. The radio operator was positioned behind the co-pilot facing aft, with his radio table in front of him. The Viscount was popular with its pilots, many of which had graduated on to the turboprop from rather more work-intensive piston-engined airliners. (Philip Jarrett Collection)

hand. The pilots sat behind a three-panel front windscreen, the central panel being completely flat, the panels either side having a slight curve. Some early Viscounts had a distinctive side panel divided horizontally by two structural members, while later production aircraft were fitted with two smaller side windows divided by a vertical frame.

Wings

Each of the Viscount's wings of equal straight-taper were divided into three sections: the inner section, which carried the Dart engines in their nacelles; a section outboard of the engines, to which were attached the wingtips. The main spar passed through all three sections at 40 per cent chord (i.e. the distance from

The 700-series prototype, G-AMAV, shows off the ingenious "petal" arrangement of its port outer Dart engine's cowling, which made working on the powerplant extremely easy for the groundcrew. The pencil-thin engine nacelles were themselves an example of superb engineering, and very much another symbol of the care and attention applied to every detail of the new airliner. (Philip Jarrett Collection)

A member of groundcrew keeps the generous flap mechanism of a Viscount clean and free from foreign object debris. When in the fully-down landing configuration, the flaps created considerable drag and a mechanism was put in place whereby if the flaps were fully extended and the throttle levers were pushed forward, the flaps would retract automatically to a position of less deflection. (The Aviation Historian Archive)

the leading edge to the spar is equal to 40 per cent of the width of the wing from leading edge to trailing edge) with secondary spars at five and 70 per cent chord. Between these two secondary spars was housed flexible crash-proof bag-type fuel tanks. On the underside of the wings numerous panels were cut to provide access to the fuel tanks, piping systems and other sundry accessories. An unusual aspect of the Viscount wing was that it had no central section or spar passing through the fuselage; instead the inner wing section was attached directly to the fuselage, the lower wing surface essentially continuing under the fuselage to form a smooth intersection.

The large double-slotted Fowler-type flaps consisted of three sections for each half-span and were mounted on internal rails. Four flap angles could be selected: 20° for take-off; 32° for maximum lift with minimum drag; 40° for approach providing some drag and considerable lift and 47° for final approach and landing. The structure of the wings was considerably beefed-up when Capital placed its order in 1954, the predominantly shorter routes of the airline meaning lower-altitude operations, which placed more stress on the airframe, and increased landing cycles. The strengthened wings would become a standard fit on all 800-series Viscounts.

Flying controls

Apart from the flaps, which were actuated by an electric motor, the flying controls were operated by means of push/pull rods and levers, the rods running beneath the cabin floor on the port side. Closed cable and tie-rod circuits from handwheels in the cockpit operated the rudder and elevator trim tabs, whereas the aileron trim-tab was electrically operated.

Undercarriage

The Viscount was fitted with a hydraulic system to raise and lower the tricycle undercarriage, which incorporated a double-wheeled single-leg nosewheel and a pair of mainwheels, also with double-wheels, which retracted forward into the inner engine nacelles. A single double-acting jack retracted each undercarriage unit, a hook on the undercarriage legs engaging with a link to draw the doors shut as the wheels retracted. Nosewheel steering was achieved by means of two hydraulic jacks mounted halfway down the nosewheel leg, which were connected to small handwheels in the cockpit, one for each pilot.

The V.790 Local Service Viscount

In early 1958 Vickers announced a version of the Viscount specially adapted for use by what it referred to as "local service operators" — essentially short-route carriers which needed an aircraft that could offer high speed at low altitude, sufficiently strengthened to cope with more frequent landings and higher landing weights. This short-route variant would be a 700-series Viscount with increased passenger accommodation (up to 65) and a number of features which would enable self-sufficient services away from major airport facilities, including integral airstairs and increased battery capacity, thus allowing the most rapid turnaround time possible. Owing to the lower altitudes the new variant was intended to operate at, the cabin pressure differential could also be lowered to 4·5lb/in^2 rather than the standard 6·5lb/in^2. Dart 506s were specified for reasons of reduced cost and slightly lighter weight. This "stretched-down" Viscount was given the designation V.790, but despite an active marketing campaign by Vickers, which claimed seat-mile costs some ten per cent lower than those of the DC-3, no orders were forthcoming and the variant was abandoned without a single example being built.

The Viscount's port double-mainwheel undercarriage unit. The majority of Viscounts were fitted with an anti-skid braking system, in which the mechanism is able to sense the sudden slowing-down of the aircraft's mainwheels preceding a skid, and momentarily release the brake, thus avoiding any loss of control as a result of skidding. This meant that the pilot could stand on the brakes fairly hard without having to worry about skidding, although it was still recommended that the system not be tried to its limits!
(Philip Jarrett Collection)

A rare photograph of Chester-built Vickers Wellington X LN715 fitted with a pair of Dart R.Da 1 turboprops in 1948. Following its use as an engine test-bed this Wellington was eventually retired from RAF service in 1951, having earned the distinction of being the first aircraft to fly powered entirely by Darts.
(Philip Jarrett Collection)

The dependable Dart

Arguably the key to the Viscount's success, Rolls-Royce's Dart turboprop engine initially showed little sign of fulfilling its future promise as one of the world's most successful and reliable powerplants. In the wake of pure-jet engine advances made during the war, it was concluded that the same essential principle of compressing and burning air could be employed to drive a propeller shaft rather than simply exiting through the exhaust at speed to provide pure thrust. It would be a far more elegant method of turning a prop than that used in noisy, dirty piston engines, which by this time were nearing the end of their development potential.

By the time the war ended Rolls-Royce was already exploring the possibilities of a turboprop, having begun work on a development of the Derwent turbojet, the Trent, which was first run in June 1944. The larger and more powerful Clyde was test-run for the first time the following year, and provided valuable experience for Rolls-Royce's Lionel Haworth and his team, who set about creating what would become the Dart. With the fitting of a pair of Trents in Gloster Meteor I EE227, the first iteration of the turboprop concept first flew in September 1945, yielding much useful information for the development of the gas turbine.

The following year work began in earnest on what would become the Dart, initially designated RB.53, the early version incorporating a two-stage centrifugal compressor, seven combustion chambers and a two-stage turbine. Results were initially disappointing, the new engine providing only 600 s.h.p. rather than the desired output of at least 1,000 s.h.p. The engine was overweight by some 30 per cent too, the original design target calling for a weight of 700lb. Nothing daunted, Rolls-Royce persevered with the R.Da 1, as the RB.53 was redesignated, and by mid-1947 had managed to reduce the engine's weight and increased its output to a respectable 1,125 e.h.p. (equivalent horsepower, a measurement comprising both the shaft horsepower – s.h.p. – and residual jet-thrust component). That October an R.Da 1 was fitted to the nose of Lancaster I NG465, trials of which proved encouraging, and a pair of Darts was also fitted to Vickers Wellington X LN715, which became the first aircraft to fly entirely under Dart power. Despite early misgivings in various quarters about the powerplant, Vickers was optimistic about the Dart, which was rugged, easy to maintain and able to

provide comparatively high speeds at altitudes above bad weather.

As an experiment to test the Dart operationally, BEA fitted a pair of its Douglas DC-3s — G-ALXN and G-AMDB — with Dart 505s in the summer of 1951 for use on some of its cargo routes. The first turboprop-powered aircraft to be put into revenue-earning service, the pair of Dart-Dakotas operated on intended Viscount routes both at home and abroad during 1951–53, both ultimately being returned to piston power to resume routine airline service. This experiment provided invaluable data on turboprop operations both for BEA and Vickers, and helped establish the Dart as a viable and desirable powerplant with a future.

The Dart would go on to become a world-beater, its variants of increasing power and efficiency providing motive power not only for every version of the Viscount, but numerous other civil and military aircraft, including the Armstrong Whitworth Argosy, Avro 748, Fokker F-27, Grumman Gulfstream I, Breguet Alizé and Japan's NAMC YS-11, among others.

Although the Dart had shown great promise when fitted to the Lancaster and Wellington test-beds, there was no information available on how it would cope with operational service. As a result a pair of BEA Dakotas, G-AMDB (named *RMA Claude Johnson*) and G-ALXN, were fitted with a pair of Dart 505s and, instead of undertaking a time-consuming test programme, were incorporated into regular BEA freight services. By the end of the trial period G-ALXN had flown more than 530hr under Dart power, with G-AMDB accruing nearly 670hr with the new powerplant. Both were re-fitted with piston engines and continued to ply their trade for BEA.
(The Aviation Historian Archive)

VICKERS VISCOUNT DATA

	V.630	V.700-series	V.800-series
Dimensions			
Span	89ft 0in (27m)	93ft 8½in (28·5m)	93ft 8½in (28·5m)
Length	74ft 6in (22·7m)	81ft 2in (24·7m)	85ft 0in (25·9m)
(with radar)	—	81ft 10in (24·9m)	85ft 8in (26·1m)
Height (to top of fin)	—	26ft 9in (8·1m)	26ft 9in (8·1m)
Tailplane span	—	37ft 0in (11·27m)	37ft 0in (11·27m)
Tailplane dihedral	15°	15°	15°
Fuselage width	—	128in (3·25m)	128in (3·25m)
Propeller diameter	—	120in (3m)	120in (3m)
Wing area	—	963ft² (89·5m²)	963ft² (89·5m²)
Wheelbase	—	24ft 10½in (7·6m)	28ft 8½in (8·75m)
Wheeltrack	—	23ft 10in (7·3m)	—
Weights			
Empty	27,000lb (12,247kg)	(V.700D) 37,918lb (17,199kg)	(V.810) 43,200lb (19,595kg)
Maximum take-off	45,000lb (20,411kg)	(V.700D) 64,500lb (29,256kg)	(V.810) 72,500lb (32,885kg)
Maximum landing	40,000lb (18,144kg)	(V.700D) 58,500lb (26,535kg)	(V.810) 62,000lb (28,123kg)
Performance			
Maximum cruise speed	300 m.p.h. (483km/h)	(V.700D) 334 m.p.h. (538km/h)	(V.810) 365 m.p.h. (587km/h)
Landing speed with full flaps	114 m.p.h. (183km/h)	(V.700D) 132 m.p.h. (212km/h)	(V.810) 137 m.p.h. (220km/h)
Climb	1,100ft/min (335m/min)	(V.700D) 1,400ft/min (427m/min)	(V.810) 1,650ft/min (503m/min)
Service ceiling	—	(V.700D) 27,500ft (8,382m)	(V.810) 27,000ft (8,230m)
Normal range with max payload and normal reserves	700 miles (1,127km)	(V.700D) 1,330 miles (2,140km)	(V.810) 1,275 miles (2,052km)

CHAPTER 5

The final variants

THE NEXT DEVELOPMENT of the ubiquitous Viscount was to be an interim variant, essentially an 800-series fitted with yet another iteration of the Dart. In 1956 the two-stage turbine Dart, as fitted to all Viscounts up to this point, had reached the end of its development life. Rolls-Royce saw continued potential in the powerplant, however, and designed a three-stage turbine version which would provide increased shaft horsepower. This new Dart variant, the R.Da 7 (Mk 520), was capable of some 1,890 e.h.p., which BEA felt could be accommodated in the V.802, the stretched Viscount having the necessary structural reserves. Designated V.806, 19 examples of the new faster variant were ordered by BEA in January 1956, to be fitted with a mixed-class interior with 16 seats in the first-class rear cabin, where noise levels were lowest, and a 42-seat forward tourist-class section.

The first V.806, registered G-AOYF, was originally intended to serve with BEA

A contemporary promotional brochure for Continental Airlines showing a rather oddly-proportioned Viscount on its opening page. Most airlines were keen to emphasise that the aircraft was "jet-powered", hence the type being referred to here as "The Jet Power Viscount II". (David H. Stringer Collection)

The first V.806, G-AOYF (c/n 255) made its maiden flight at Weybridge, bearing the legend "Vickers Viscount 806–810" along the fuselage, on August 9, 1957. The aircraft was fitted with an experimental "horn-balance" rudder, in which the rudder unit included the fin cap, as seen in this publicity photograph, but during flight trials over West Sussex there was a loud bang, after which the rudder became unserviceable; on landing it was found to be buckled and stress creases were found in the rear fuselage. After further testing on another airframe, in which the rudder buckled again, the idea was abandoned. (The Aviation Historian Archive)

with the name *Michael Faraday,* but it was retained by Vickers as a trials and certification aircraft for further Viscount developments, including the V.810, of which more later. With the legend "Vickers Viscount 806–810" emblazoned along its upper fuselage, G-AOYF made its maiden flight on August 9, 1957, the variant being allocated its CoA the following month.

The entry of BEA's V.806s into service in early 1958 coincided with the delivery

Named *RMA John Napier* in honour of the Scottish discoverer of logarithms, V.806 G-AOYP (c/n 265) is seen here at Heathrow in 1958, before BEA's new "red square" colour scheme was applied in March 1959. One of the longest-serving Viscounts, G-AOYP went on to operate with Cambrian Airways, British Airways, British Air Ferries/British World Airlines, Virgin Atlantic Airways and Parcelforce, as well as several lease periods with other companies. This dependable workhorse was sold to an owner in South Africa in 1997, finally ending its flying career after nearly 40 years. (The Aviation Historian Archive)

In November 1955 the New Zealand National Airways Corporation (NZNAC) ordered three V.807s, including ZK-BRF (c/n 283), which was named *City of Christchurch*. Fitted with Dart 510 engines, ZK-BRF was delivered to the airline at Christchurch, New Zealand, on March 23, 1959, flying its first service on April 6 the same year. It is seen here in a later NZNAC scheme, applied from 1968. The aircraft was withdrawn from service in July 1974, and the following year was donated to the Ferrymead Museum of Science & Technology at Christchurch, where it remains on display in 2018. (The Aviation Historian Archive)

of the first of five Dart 520-powered V.807s to New Zealand National Airways Corporation (NZNAC), the Viscount offering a quantum leap from NZNAC's ageing fleet of DC-3s. Irish national airline Aer Lingus had a requirement for a stretched Viscount with excellent short/medium-range performance for its busier runs to the UK and mainland Europe and ordered eight 520-powered V.808s in May 1956, the first of these being delivered in May 1957. These three airlines were the only three to operate the 520-powered variant, a total of 30 of which were built. The 802/806 variants showed the inherent development potential of the Viscount a decade after the first prototype had flown, although a total of only 67 were built, all except the New Zealand examples being operated by European airlines. There was

Named *Colmcille* in honour of the 6th-Century Irish abbot (St Columba), V.808 EI-AKL (c/n 423) was delivered to Aer Lingus in March 1959. The Irish national airline adopted at least six different colour schemes between 1954 and the mid-1960s, mostly variations on a green and white theme, this iteration being one of the most attractive, with a green upper fuselage, white cheat line and cockpit and bare-metal undersides. The white fin carried the national flag and six green lines overlaid with a green shamrock in a white circle, with the aircraft's registration beneath. This aircraft went on to serve with Sultan of Oman's Air Force during 1973–76 and ended its career in Zaïre in the mid-1980s. (Mike Hooks)

another variant to come, however, which would prove to be the ultimate Viscount both in terms of its performance and its place in the type's long history.

"The best Viscount yet . . ."

While the Dart 520-powered 806/807/808 series offered good performance and excellent economics on shorter-range high-density inter-city routes, a number of airlines expressed a desire for a variant offering the same capacity but greater range, ideally at higher speeds. Leading the field of enquiries was American operator Continental Airlines, which had shown interest in the Viscount back in 1954, but which had never placed an order for the type. Based in Denver, Colorado, located in the Rocky Mountains, some 5,000ft (1,525m) above sea level and prone to very hot summers and freezing winters, Continental's requirements were somewhat demanding. The airline served not only local routes but also important long-distance transcontinental routes from the Great Lakes and the Midwest to the West Coast. Initially interested in the 800-series after KLM's purchase of its V.803s, Continental let Vickers know that more power and greater range would be required to fulfil its requirements, although the capacity of the stretched 800-series was about right.

As a result, Vickers and Rolls-Royce set about tweaking the Viscount further, confident that other operators with similar requirements would be interested in a faster, longer-range version. At the same time Vickers would use the opportunity to clear up as many of the type's deficiencies as possible without engaging in a full redesign. Clearly the key to this next development would be another step in the evolution of the Dart, which had already been upgraded to a three-stage turbine engine in the form of the 520. Rolls-Royce accordingly set to work, taking the 520 and adding a recalibrated fuel-control unit, increased flame temperature, new trapezoidal-planform propellers and various other modifications to create the Dart 525, capable of some 2,100 e.h.p., nearly twice that of the Dart 502 that had powered the V.630 prototype.

The greater power of the new Dart 525 meant that the airframe in which it was to be fitted would need to be strengthened, with more structure in the wings to meet higher landing weights and a beefing-up of the fuselage, tail and flying controls to cater for the additional speed and power. A brand new wing was considered, as was a radically redesigned fuselage, but it became clear that

This 1959 advertisement extols the virtues of Continental Airlines' "Gold Carpet" service, which saw customers served champagne and filet mignon steak while making the most of the Viscount's panoramic windows. As the copy says: "How long since you've been hailed as a conquering hero? Never? Then come aboard a Continental Jet Power Viscount II . . . you're always a Caesar to us. Unless, of course, you're Cleopatra". Bonkers, but fun. (David H. Stringer Collection)

In December 1955 Bob Six (left), the President of Continental Airlines, signed a contract with Vickers' Managing Director George Edwards for 15 V.812s, which were delivered between May 1958 and May 1959. The V.812s, powered by Dart 525s and configured in a 52-seat + four-seat rear lounge layout, were dubbed "Viscount IIs" in Continental service, so as to distinguish them from Capital Airlines' 700-series examples. (Mike Hooks Collection)

the existing wing could be reworked to do the job. This strengthening would also build in even more development potential, further evolution of the Dart allowing the possibility of a 400 m.p.h. (643km/h)-plus Viscount, already earmarked for development by Vickers as the 840-series.

The installation of the 525 would require the strengthening of the nacelles, and rudder authority was increased with a control modification which allowed greater deflection. The gap between the rudder and the fin, and the elevators and the tailplane, were also modified to remedy the accumulation of snow – a lesson

A classic scene at Amsterdam-Schiphol in April 1964, with Lufthansa Viscount V.814 D-ANIZ (c/n 344) sharing the ramp with V.803s of Dutch national airline KLM. Lufthansa operated a total of 11 Viscounts, three of them being long-leased to the company's charter associate Condor Flugdienst during 1961–69. Although Lufthansa ordered Boeing 737s in the mid-1960s to replace the Viscounts, the latter remained in service with the airline, mostly on domestic and back-up duties, until 1971. (Mike Hooks)

Calling on the Viscount's capabilities under "hot and high" conditions, South African Airways (SAA) ordered seven V.813s in March 1956 to replace its Lockheed Constellations and Douglas DC-3s and DC-4s. The airline very quickly felt the benefit of the "Viscount jump", turning an ongoing loss on its domestic routes with the piston-engined airliners to a substantial profit within seven months of acquiring the new turboprop. This example, ZS-CDX (c/n 350), served with SAA until it was sold to British Midland Airways in 1972. It still survives as an exhibit outside a nightclub in Belgium. (Ken Smy via The Aviation Historian Archive)

learned during airline operations. Despite these measures, the Dart 525s would still have to be de-rated to around 1,750 s.h.p, as the engines would provide an unrequired surfeit of power, which would cost fuel – always a key concern for airlines. The dimensions of the earlier 800-series Viscount would remain exactly the same on the 810, as the new variant was designated.

Continental was impressed with what it saw and ordered 15 V.812s "off the drawing board" in December 1955. South African Airways, German airline Lufthansa and Pakistan International Airlines followed suit the following spring with orders for seven V.813s, ten V.814s and three V.815s respectively. The first V.806, G-AOYF, was

In May 1956 Pakistan International Airlines (PIA) placed an order for three V.815s (with another two ordered in 1959), the first of which, AP-AJC (c/n 335), named *City of Karachi*, was delivered to Karachi in January 1959. This aircraft operated the first PIA turboprop service on the last day of that month when it flew from Karachi to Delhi, but had only a short career as it was written off in a non-fatal landing accident during a training flight at Rawalpindi on May 18, 1959. (The Aviation Historian Archive)

fitted with Dart 525s and departed Wisley for tropical trials in Africa on September 21, 1957. After a month of trials at Salisbury, Rhodesia (now Zimbabwe), during which the Viscount suffered quickly-repaired damage in a landing accident, 'Yankee Foxtrot' moved on to Johannesburg, where on October 20, it swung off the runway on landing. There were no injuries, but the aircraft was damaged beyond repair, although it was returned to the UK and used to form the basis of V.806 G-APOX, which was delivered to BEA in 1959.

The first 810-series Viscount built as such, G-AOYV, was painted in Continental colours and made its first flight on December 23, 1957, from Weybridge. The trials programme was completed with very little trouble, despite the fact that the 810 was the first variant to incorporate significant construction changes, and the 810 received its American FAA certification in April 1958. The following month Continental launched its Viscount services with a Chicago–Los Angeles flight on May 28, a mere five months after the first flight of G-AOYV. The type proved a great success for Continental, which initially operated them on a reduced-capacity first-class service, and within a year of the type entering service the airline reported a $4m upturn in revenue. With the arrival of jet-powered Boeing 707s in the summer of 1959, the V.812s' luxurious first-class interiors were gradually supplanted by a five-abreast all-economy configuration.

More orders for the 525-powered 800-series followed, including V.816s for Trans-Australia Airlines, V.818s for Cubana, V.827s for Brazilian airline VASP, V.828s for All Nippon Airways in Japan, V.831s for Airwork, V.832s for Australian operator

Originally built for Hunting-Clan as one of its three V.833s, G-APTC (c/n 425) is seen here at Heathrow in August 1961 bearing the markings of Central African Airways, while operating as part of British United Airways' "Skycoach" service to Central Africa during 1960–61. The aircraft was sold to Arkia Israel Inland Airways in 1969, but was written off after a taxying accident at Tel Aviv in October 1969. (John Havers via The Aviation Historian Archive)

Viscount V.816 VH-TVR (c/n 435), named *John Murray* in honour of the 18th-Century Australian explorer, was exhibited in Trans-Australia Airlines (TAA) colours at the 1959 SBAC show at Farnborough, as seen here. Although TAA did take delivery of two V.816s, VH-TVR was not one of them and was converted to the sole V.836, N40N, for the Union Carbide & Carbon Corporation in the USA in the spring of 1960. It would later see service as the Royal Australian Air Force's A6-435. (The Aviation Historian Archive)

Ansett-ANA, V.833s for Hunting-Clan, V.837s for Austrian Airlines and V.838s for Ghana Airways. The final Viscount order was for six 810-series examples for the Civil Aviation Administration of China (CAAC) – the first order placed by Communist China for a Western aircraft – which received its V.843s from July 1963. As China was subject to American trade sanctions at the time (which created political headaches for Vickers), all items originating from the USA in the Chinese Viscounts had to be replaced with British components, including hydraulic, navigation and electronic equipment.

Having previously operated four V.779s leased from Norway's Fred Olsen Air Transport from 1958, Austrian Airlines (formed that year) acquired six V.837s in 1960, at which point the 700-series Viscounts were returned to Fred Olsen. This V.837, OE-LAF (named *Joseph Haydn*), seen during a photo sortie before its delivery in February 1960, was destroyed less than eight months after its first flight when it crashed into trees during a second approach to Moscow's Sheremetyevo airport in poor weather on September 26, 1960. Five crew and 25 passengers of the 37 persons on aboard were killed. (The Aviation Historian Archive)

VICKERS VISCOUNT VARIANTS

THE FOLLOWING is a list of the series numbers applied by Vickers to the Viscount variants supplied by the company to individual customers. Other serial numbers were allocated to Viscount projects which were not proceeded with and remained unbuilt. The latter are not listed here.

Type No	Powerplant	No built	Customer
600-series			
V.630 (G-AHRF)	4 x Dart RDa 1 (Mk 502)	1	Ministry of Supply
V.663 (VX217)	2 x Tay RTa 1 turbojets	1	Ministry of Supply
700-series			
V.700 (G-AMAV)	4 x Dart RDa 3 (Mk 505)	1	Ministry of Supply
V.701	4 x Dart RDa 3 (Mk 506)	27	British European Airways
V.702	4 x Dart RDa 3 (Mk 506)	4	British West Indian Airways (BWIA)
V.707	4 x Dart RDa 3 (Mk 505/506)	4	Aer Lingus
V.708	4 x Dart RDa 3 (Mk 505/506)	12	Air France
V.720	4 x Dart RDa 3 (Mk 506)	7	Trans-Australia Airways
V.723 (IU-683)	4 x Dart RDa 3 (Mk 506)	1	Indian Air Force (part-VIP interior)
V.724	4 x Dart RDa 3 (Mk 506)	15	Trans-Canada Air Lines
V.730 (IU-684)	4 x Dart RDa 3 (Mk 506)	1	Indian Air Force (full VIP interior)
V.732	4 x Dart RDa 3 (Mk 506)	3	Hunting-Clan Air Transport
V.734 (J751)	4 x Dart RDa 3 (Mk 506)	1	Pakistan Air Force (VIP)
V.735	4 x Dart RDa 3 (Mk 506)	3	Iraqi Airways
V.736	4 x Dart RDa 3 (Mk 506)	2	Fred Olsen Flyselskap A/S
V.737 (CF-GXK)	4 x Dart RDa 3 (Mk 506)	1	Canadian Dept of Transportation
V.739/739A/739B	4 x Dart RDa 3 (Mk 506)	6	Misrair
V.742D	4 x Dart RDa 6 (Mk 510)	1	Intended for Braathens-SAFE Air Transport, but delivered to Brazilian Air Force as FAB-2100
V.744	4 x Dart RDa 3 (Mk 506)	3	Capital Airlines
V.745/745D*	4 x Dart RDa 3/6 (Mk 506/510)	60	Capital Airlines
V.747	4 x Dart RDa 3 (Mk 506)	2	Butler Air Transport
V.748D	4 x Dart RDa 6 (Mk 510)	5	Central African Airways
V.749	4 x Dart RDa 3 (Mk 506)	3	Linea Aeropostal Venelozana (LAV)
V.754D	4 x Dart RDa 6 (Mk 510)	8	BOAC/Middle East Airways
V.755D	4 x Dart RDa 6 (Mk 510)	3	Ordered by Airwork; delivered to Cubana
V.756D	4 x Dart RDa 6 (Mk 510)	7	Trans-Australia Airlines
V.757	4 x Dart RDa 3 (Mk 506)	36	Trans-Canada Airlines
V.759D	4 x Dart RDa 6 (Mk 510)	2	Ordered by Hunting-Clan but transferred to Icelandair
V.760D	4 x Dart RDa 6 (Mk 510)	2	BOAC/ Hong Kong Airways
V.761D	4 x Dart RDa 6 (Mk 510)	3	Union of Burma Airways
V.763D (YS-09C)	4 x Dart RDa 6 (Mk 510)	1	Ordered by Howard Hughes; delivered to TACA
V.764D	4 x Dart RDa 6 (Mk 510)	3	US Steel Corporation
V.765D (N306)	4 x Dart RDa 6 (Mk 510)	1	Standard Oil Corporation
V.768D	4 x Dart RDa 6 (Mk 510)	10	Indian Airlines
V.769D	4 x Dart RDa 6 (Mk 510)	3	Primeras Líneas Uruguayas de Navegación Aérea (PLUNA)
V.772	4 x Dart RDa 3 (Mk 506)	4	BOAC/BWIA
V.773 (YI-ACU)	4 x Dart RDa 3 (Mk 506)	1	Iraqi Airways
V.776D (G-APNF)	4 x Dart RDa 6 (Mk 510)	1	Kuwait Oil Company
V.779D	4 x Dart RDa 6 (Mk 510)	4	Fred Olsen Flyselskap A/S; leased to other operators
V.781D ("150")	4 x Dart RDa 6 (Mk 510)	1	South African Air Force (VIP)
V.782D	4 x Dart RDa 6 (Mk 510)	3	Iranian Airlines
V.784D	4 x Dart RDa 6 (Mk 510)	3	Philippine Airlines
V.785D	4 x Dart RDa 6 (Mk 510)	10	Linee Aeree Italiane/Alitalia
V.786D	4 x Dart RDa 6 (Mk 510)	3	Lloyd Aereo Colombiana
V.789D (FAB-2101)	4 x Dart RDa 6 (Mk 510)	1	Brazilian Air Force (VIP)

V.793D (CF-RBC)	4 x Dart RDa 6 (Mk 510)	1	Royal Bank of Canada
V.794D	4 x Dart RDa 6 (Mk 510)	4	Turk Hava Yollari
V.797D (CF-DTA)	4 x Dart RDa 6 (Mk 510)	1	Canadian Dept of Transportation
V.798D	4 x Dart RDa 6 (Mk 510)	10	Northeast Airlines
800-series			
V.802	4 x Dart RDa 6 (Mk 510)	24	British European Airways
V.803	4 x Dart RDa 6 (Mk 510)	9	KLM
V.804	4 x Dart RDa 6 (Mk 510)	3	Transair
V.805	4 x Dart RDa 6 (Mk 510)	2	Eagle Aviation
V.806	4 x Dart RDa 7 (Mk 520)	19	British European Airways
V.806A (G-AOYF)	4 x Dart RDa 7 (Mk 520)	1	V.806 prototype and development aircraft for 810-series
V.807	4 x Dart RDa 7 (Mk 520)	4	New Zealand National Airways Corporation
V.808	4 x Dart RDa 7 (Mk 520)	6	Aer Lingus
V.810 (G-AOYV)	4 x Dart RDa 7/1 (Mk 525)	1	Vickers; 810-series prototype
V.812	4 x Dart RDa 7/1 (Mk 525)	15	Continental Airlines
V.813	4 x Dart RDa 7/1 (Mk 525)	7	South African Airways
V.814	4 x Dart RDa 7/1 (Mk 525)	10	Lufthansa
V.815	4 x Dart RDa 7/1 (Mk 525)	5	Pakistan International Airlines
V.816	4 x Dart RDa 7/1 (Mk 525)	2	Trans-Australia Airways
V.818	4 x Dart RDa 7/1 (Mk 525)	3	Cubana
V.827	4 x Dart RDa 7/1 (Mk 525)	6	VASP
V.828	4 x Dart RDa 7/1 (Mk 525)	9	All Nippon Airways
V.831	4 x Dart RDa 7/1 (Mk 525)	3	2 for Airwork; 1 for Sudan Airways
V.832	4 x Dart RDa 7/1 (Mk 525)	4	Ansett-ANA
V.833	4 x Dart RDa 7/1 (Mk 530)	3	Hunting-Clan
V.835 (N500T)	4 x Dart RDa 7/1 (Mk 525)	1	Tennessee Gas Transmission Corporation (VIP conversion from undelivered Cubana V.818)
V.836 (N40N)	4 x Dart RDa 7/1 (Mk 525)	1	Union Carbide & Carbon Corporation; later used by RAAF as A6-435
V.837	4 x Dart RDa 7/1 (Mk 525)	6	Austrian Airlines
V.838	4 x Dart RDa 7/1 (Mk 525)	3	Ghana Airways
V.839	4 x Dart RDa 7/1 (Mk 525)	1	Iranian Government
V.843	4 x Dart RDa 7/1 (Mk 525)	6	Civil Aviation Administration of China
TOTAL		**444**	

*The D suffix denotes aircraft built to American FAA certification standards

CHAPTER 6

Into Uniform

AS THE REPUTATION of the Viscount as the "must-have" item for the world's short- and medium-haul operators grew, so did the interest of military and official government organisations, which would value the thoroughly modern airliner's speed, cost-effectiveness and high level of comfort. The first air arm to acquire the Viscount was the Indian Air Force (IAF), which placed an order for two 700-series aircraft in November 1953. It was announced that both aircraft would serve with the IAF's Communications Squadron, and would be based at Palan, near Delhi. The first to fly, designated a V.793, made its maiden flight from Weybridge on November 8, 1955, and was handed over to the IAF the following month with the military serial IU-683, named *Pushpaka*. Configured as a general duties transport aircraft, IU-683 accommodated 28 passengers in the rear cabin with a seven-seat VIP forward section that incorporated a conference table.

The second IAF Viscount, IU-684, was configured as a dedicated VIP transport with a ten-seat VIP layout with separate sleeping quarters and a lounge area, and was accordingly given a separate designation, V.730. Having made its first flight from Weybridge on December 14, 1955, the aircraft was named *Raj Humsa* and also arrived in India in January 1956. Both were much used to fly high-ranking government officials around the country for the next decade, and were withdrawn from service in 1966, both being sold on to the Indian Airlines Corporation.

Originally built as a V.838 for Ghana Airways, with which it served during 1961–65, Viscount XT661 is seen here in the distinctive "raspberry ripple" colours it wore from 1977 while operating with the Royal Aircraft Establishment (RAE) at Thurleigh. Used extensively for radar-jamming trials of the UK air-defence system, the aircraft was fitted with pods to house equipment beneath the aircraft. (Mike Hooks)

Following in its neighbours footsteps, Pakistan ordered the sole V.734, J751 (c/n 83), in 1955. The 100th production Viscount built, the aircraft made its first flight on February 29, 1956, and was handed over to the Pakistan Air Force on March 20 the same year, as seen here. Note the badge on the nose bearing the legend "President of Pakistan"; wing-mounted "slipper" tanks outboard of Nos 1 and 4 engines were also fitted as standard. In April 1970 J751 was sold to the Civil Aviation Administration of China, registered B-414 and used as a VIP transport by Chinese government officials. (Philip Jarrett Collection)

Pakistan

The second military operator to place an order for the Viscount was India's neighbour Pakistan, which announced the purchase of one V.734 in April 1955. To be used in the VIP transport role, the aircraft was configured to accommodate 24 people in three compartments. The forward VIP saloon incorporated two beds, two aft-facing chairs and side tables; the central section comprised four-abreast seating for 16 passengers, four of which faced aft, the remainder facing forward. The rear section provided seating for six staff, aft of which was a galley with a cooker and a refrigerator. Having made its maiden flight on February 29, 1956, the Viscount was handed over to the Pakistan Air Force (PAF) on March 20 the same year with the serial J751 and fitted with a pair of extended-range "slipper" fuel tanks outboard of the outer Darts. The aircraft provided sterling service for the PAF until the spring of 1970, when it was sold to the Civil Aviation Administration of China.

Brazil

In October 1956 the Forca Aérea Brasileira (FAB — Brazilian Air Force) negotiated with Vickers to acquire a V.742D originally ordered by Braathens-SAFE, but which the Norwegian airline found surplus to its needs. Accordingly the Viscount was painted in full FAB markings with the serial FAB-2100 (the hyphen was subsequently removed) and the following month the aircraft was handed over to the FAB at Hurn. After being fitted with a VIP interior to accommodate 22 passengers, with separate sleeping quarters and a radio-operator's station, it was delivered to the FAB in Brazil in February 1957.

The same year the FAB ordered a second Viscount, which made its first flight from Hurn on December 1, 1957, to become FAB 2101, the sole V.789D. Handed over to the FAB at the end of that month, the aircraft was also equipped with a VIP interior and remained in the UK for crew training until October 1958, when it was delivered to Brazil.

In December 1957 the Brazilian military serial system changed and FAB 2100 was re-serialled C-90 2100 (the C-90 prefix being the FAB's designation for the type). On its arrival the following year, FAB 2101 was re-serialled C-90 2101, and both operated on national and international flights until C-90 2100 was written off during a heavy landing at Rio de Janeiro on December 8, 1967. The second FAB Viscount was withdrawn from service in 1970 and later became a museum exhibit.

The Forca Aérea Brasileira (FAB – Brazilian Air Force) operated two Viscounts, the first, V.742D FAB-2100 (c/n 141), being acquired in November 1956. The erroneous hyphen in the serial was removed shortly thereafter, as seen here at Hurn, and the aircraft operated in the VIP role until a landing accident ended its career in December 1967. The FAB's other Viscount was V.789D FAB 2101 (c/n 345), which entered FAB service in October 1958, by which time it had been re-serialled C-90 2101. It was withdrawn from use in 1970 and exists today as an exhibit at an air museum in Rio de Janeiro. (Philip Jarrett Collection)

Built at Hurn, the sole V.781D for the South African Air Force (SAAF) made its first flight on May 18, 1958, and was delivered to the SAAF in a gleaming colour scheme of bare-metal and white cabin roof the following June. When handed over to the SAAF, serial 150 (c/n 280) was carrying a large consignment of Viscount spares which were apparently never used, and were discovered in the UK in 2010. Many of these parts have subsequently been used in Viscount restoration projects around the world.
(Ken Smy via The Aviation Historian Archive)

South Africa

Seeing in the Viscount a perfect vehicle in which to transport senior officials and military personnel around South Africa and its neighbouring countries, the South African Air Force (SAAF) ordered a single V.781D with Dart 510s, the aircraft making its first flight from Hurn on May 18, 1958. A month later the VIP-configured Viscount, serialled 150, was delivered to the SAAF, with which it operated with No 21 Sqn. In August 1984 the aircraft was put on the South African civil register as ZS-LFR, but it continued to operate on government and military duties with No 44 Sqn. Up until the time it was sold to a new owner in Zaïre in 1991, it was the last Viscount still serving with its original operator.

The secondhand military operators

A number of other air arms also operated the Viscount, acquiring secondhand examples for various duties. The RAF's Empire Test Pilots School (ETPS) acquired the first of its two Viscounts in January 1962. An ex-Capital V.744, which had also served with All Nippon Airways, XR801 (formerly N7403 and G-APKK) was delivered to Royal Aircraft Establishment (RAE) Farnborough in January 1962, after which it departed for a tour of the USA's military test centres. Another ex-Capital machine, V.745D N7442, was acquired by the ETPS in May 1962 and was serialled XR802. Both were extensively used until their withdrawal from service in late 1971, after which both were scrapped.

Two more Viscounts were used by British test organisations. The first was ex-Austrian Airlines V.837 OE-LAG, which was given the British military serial XT575 and operated by the Royal Radar & Signals Establishment at RAE Pershore, where it arrived in August 1964, and where it was fitted with a large belly-mounted radome for anti-submarine warfare trials. The second, XT661, was an ex-Ghana Airways V.838, and arrived at Pershore in late February 1965, also being fitted with various belly-mounted pods for electronic trials. Both played an important part in the development of the ill-fated BAC TSR.2 strike aircraft's electronic systems and undertook extensive trials for the Panavia Tornado GR.1 programme, before being transferred to the RAE at Thurleigh in 1977. In

Following service with Capital Airlines in the USA as N7403 and with Japanese airline All Nippon Airways with British registration G-APKK, V.744 c/n 89 was acquired by the Empire Test Pilots School (ETPS) at Farnborough, where it was delivered with the military serial XR801 in January 1962. As seen here beside the ETPS hangar at Farnborough in September 1964, the Viscount was painted in a predominantly white colour scheme with aluminium paint undersurfaces, a blue cheat line roundels and fin flashes, plus a spark emblem on the dorsal fillet. It was retired from service in October 1971 and was ultimately broken up. (Mike Hooks)

1991 the aircraft were transferred to the Defence Research Agency, but both were retired shortly afterwards after more than two decades of arduous and extensive test work.

In August 1964 it was becoming increasingly clear to the Royal Australian Air Force (RAAF) that a modern alternative to its hard-pressed Dakotas and Convair 440s was required for the VIP transport role. Accordingly, a pair of 800-series Viscounts was ordered in July 1964. The first, serialled A6-435 in RAAF service, was a former corporate-owned Dart 525-powered V.816, which arrived in the Australian capital at the end of August the same year. The second, A6-436, also a Dart 525-powered V.816, joined the first at Canberra in October 1964. Used comparatively sparingly, both were withdrawn from service in March 1969 having accrued less than 5,000 flying hours. Perhaps unsurprisingly, both went on to have extended careers, both finding another

One of the two Viscounts operated by the Empire Test Pilots' School during 1962–71, XR802 (c/n 198) is seen here at Farnborough in April 1964. In 1970 the aircraft was repainted in a similar scheme but with a red fin and the blue spark emblem replaced with a blue version with a white outline. By the end of the following year, however, it had been released for disposal by the Ministry of Defence, and in May 1972 it was bought by Shackleton Aviation and ferried to Coventry, where it was broken up for spares. (Mike Stroud via The Aviation Historian Archive)

The first of two Viscounts to be acquired by the Royal Australian Air Force (RAAF), A6-436 (c/n 436) is seen here at Wisley after completion of its refurbishment before delivery to the RAAF in late 1964. Originally the sole V.839, EP-MRS, this aircraft was delivered to the Iranian Government in May 1961 for use as a VIP transport by the Shah, although it also served with Iranian Airways/Iranair during 1963–64. In 1965 the aircraft earned the distinction of transporting Her Majesty the Queen Mother on her Australian tour. Both of the RAAF's Viscounts went on to serve with the Sultan of Oman's Air Force from 1971. (The Aviation Historian Archive)

military home when they were acquired by the Sultan of Oman's Air Force (SOAF) in the autumn of 1971. Given the serials 501 and 502, the aircraft served with the SOAF until 1977, when both were retired from the SOAF inventory and returned to the UK, to be sold on yet again to continue their long, peripatetic careers.

The final military operator of the Viscount was the Turk Hava Kuvvetieri (THK – Turkish Air Force), which acquired three Dart 510-powered V.794Ds from Turk Hava Yollari (THY – Turkish Airlines) in March 1971. The THY machines had originally been built with a VIP conversion option, whereby the rear 28 seats could be removed to accommodate two beds and a lounge, with a table and four chairs. The forward 20 seats remained in a standard airline configuration. The three THK Viscounts were serialled according to their construction numbers, becoming 246, 430 and 431. All had been withdrawn from service by 1990.

Following its service with the RAAF, c/n 436 was acquired by the Sultan of Oman's Air Force and given the serial 502, as which it was delivered in August 1971. Seen here in Oman, the aircraft was returned in November 1976 to Hurn, from where it had made its maiden flight in September 1959, pending its onward sale to the British Aircraft Corporation, which sold it on again to Royal Swazi National Airlines as 3D-CAN in 1978. After stints with Dan-Air as G-BGLC and Air Zimbabwe as VP-WGB and later as Z-WGB, it was finally withdrawn from service at Harare, Zimbabwe, in late 1990. (The Aviation Historian Archive)

ABOVE: Having served with Turkish national airline Turk Hava Yollari for 14 years, V.794D TC-SEC (c/n 246) was one of three transferred to the Turkish Air Force during 1971–72. The Viscounts were used for general transport and VIP duties in Turkey and throughout the Eastern Mediterranean and served for nearly 20 years before being withdrawn from 1988, the last of the three, 430, soldiering on until the early 1990s, after which it was put on display at a museum at Yesilkoy, Istanbul. (The Aviation Historian Archive)

The Men from the Canadian Ministry

Although not a military operator as such, another government organisation that reaped the rewards offered by the Viscount was Canada's Department of Transportation (DoT), which took delivery of its first example of the type, the sole V.737 CF-GXK, in March 1955. Fitted with a VIP interior and integral airstairs, the Dart 506-powered aircraft made its first flight on the 15th of that month before being flown to Canada by Vickers test pilot Jock Bryce, who landed the Viscount in Ottawa on March 28. After seven months with Trans-Canada Airlines (TCA) for crew training, CF-GXK returned to service with the DoT in October 1955.

A second Viscount, originally built to a Capital Airlines V.745D order, which was ultimately not taken up, was acquired by the Canadian DoT in March 1958 and registered CF-DTA. Given the designation V.797D, the aircraft made its first post-conversion flight on March 21, 1958, and departed Hurn for Canada on November 23 that year. The DoT's third and final Viscount, former TCA V.724 CF-TGP, was delivered in September 1964, and served for nearly five years before being withdrawn from service in January 1969, having accrued some 20,150 flying hours. The other two Viscounts continued to see regular service on national and international excursions until their retirement in 1982.

Three Viscounts were operated by Canada's Department of Transport (DoT), the second of which was V.797D CF-DTA (c/n 229), seen here sporting the DoT's tasteful white and grey scheme with yellow detailing, including on the slipper tanks, at Dorval Airport in Montreal in September 1968. (Mike Stroud via The Aviation Historian Archive)

CHAPTER 7

'Twas a dark and stormy night ...

The Crash of Viscount VH-TVC, November 30, 1961

Text by Macarthur Job

AUSTRALIA'S AIRLINE NETWORK was thriving in 1961, especially on the trunk routes of the nation's two major air carriers, Trans-Australia Airlines (TAA) and Ansett-ANA. Under the eagle eye of the Department of Civil Aviation (DCA), air travel had become a model of safety and efficiency; the result of 40 years of harsh experience. However, one vital lesson remained to be learned, and it would be costly and soul-searching.

Originally built at Hurn as a V.720A, VH-TVC (c/n 46) was named *John Oxley* and delivered to Trans-Australia Airlines at Melbourne in December 1954. Shortly thereafter it was converted to V.720C configuration, which entailed a new cockpit instrumentation layout, the replacement of the needle-blade propellers with paddle-bladed props linked to an auto-synchronisation system and the fitting of Dart 510 engines. In March 1960 the aircraft was transferred to Ansett-ANA, in whose colours it is seen here at Essendon (Melbourne). (Civil Aviation Historical Society/www.airwaysmuseum.com)

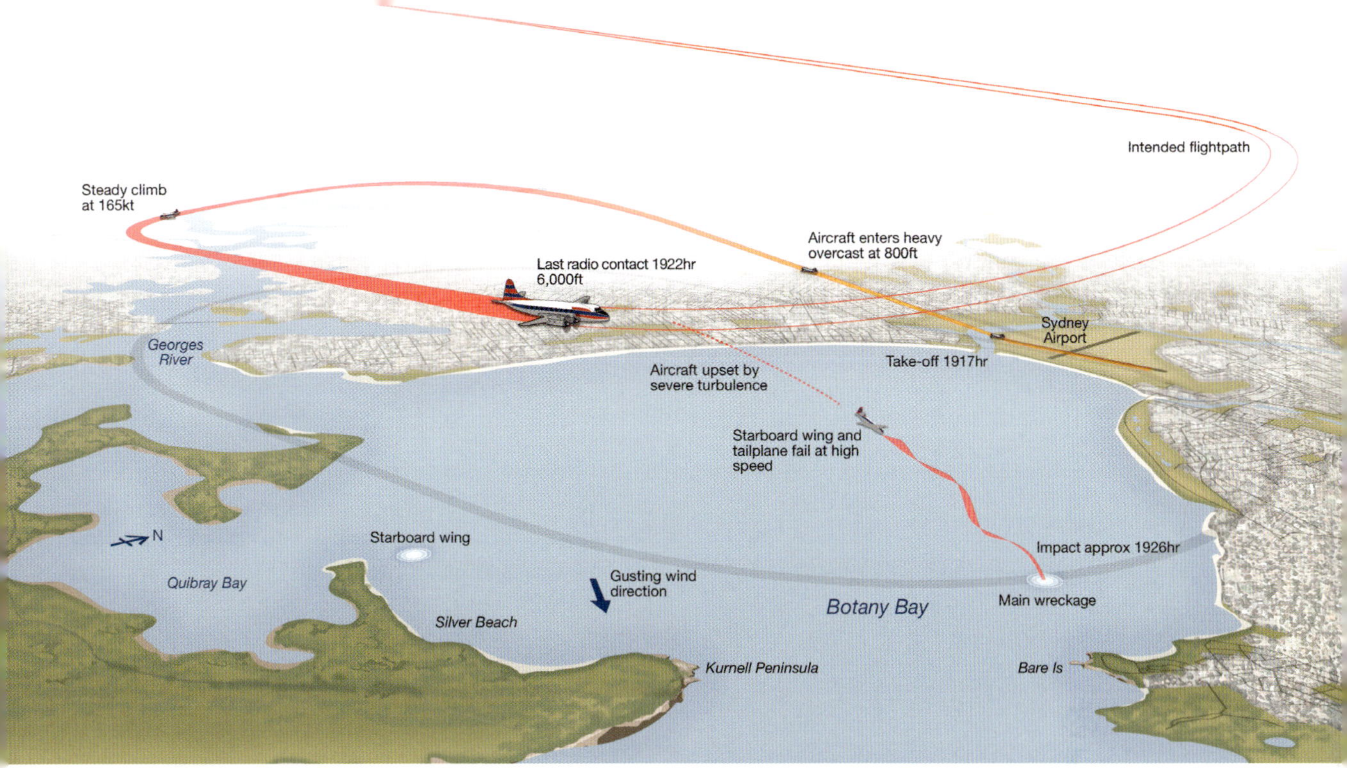

The fateful last flight of Ansett-ANA Viscount VH-TVC on November 30, 1961. Artwork by JUANITA FRANZI/AERO ILLUSTRATIONS © 2017

The schedule for Ansett-ANA Viscount V.720 VH-TVC on Thursday, November 30, 1961, was light; three trips between Sydney and Canberra, a relatively short distance of 130 miles (210km). The day-return trip to Canberra, although rough, was without incident, and 'Victor Charlie' landed back at Sydney just on 1745hr. The crew rostered for the flight back to Canberra at 1910hr comprised Capt S.A. Lindsay, First Officer B.A. Costello and stewardesses Aileen Keldie and Elizabeth Hardy.

It had been a wild day, with heavy rain, blustery westerly winds, punctuated by thunder and lightning. Towards evening, conditions seemed to be worsening. At around 1800hr Capt Lindsay went to the airport briefing office. The meteorological officer gave him the route forecast and briefed him on the active front approaching Sydney from the west. Radar returns showed cloud tops extending to 35,000ft (10,670m). Pilots were reporting exceptionally severe turbulence.

When Lindsay returned to the terminal the two stewardesses were waiting to board the Viscount, which was parked on the rainswept tarmac outside. Costello, with umbrella in hand, was making a pre-flight inspection with a despatching engineer. The two girls were joined by trainee stewardess Dagmar Schmidt, who had been part of the aircraft's crew on the late afternoon flight from Canberra.

The cabin was configured for 48 passengers, but only 11 were booked on the flight. All but two were Canberra residents; a gynæcologist at the Royal Canberra Hospital, two civil servants, an army major, three Canberra company managers, the wife of another Canberra medical practitioner and a self-employed businessman. The other two were an oil company representative and a soldier on his way to the Royal Military College.

At 1905hr Costello called Sydney tower for start-up clearance. Five minutes later the tower cleared 'TVC to Runway 25 for a south-west take-off. Because of the

The cockpit of VH-TVC, in which Capt Lindsay and First Officer Costello battled a storm of biblical proportions – and lost – on the evening of November 30, 1961. After the loss of VH-TVC it was made a legal requirement to have weather radar fitted in all civil turbine-powered aircraft in Australia. (Civil Aviation Historical Society/www.airwaysmuseum.com)

heavy cloud and rain the taxiway and runway lights were already on. The tower issued an amended airways clearance. To avoid inbound traffic this required a departure track of 244° magnetic until 37 miles (60km) from Sydney; thence to Canberra, cruising at 16,000ft (4,875m).

At 1916hr the controller cleared Victor Charlie for take-off, instructing the aircrew to maintain runway heading to 3,000ft (915m), then to turn to port to pass "over the field, not below 5,000ft [1,524m]". The aircraft took off normally, its navigation lights being lost to view as it entered heavy cloud at about 800ft (245m). The tower controller logged the time as 1917hr local.

Five minutes later the controller offered the aircraft a choice of two departure tracks; the original track Lindsay had nominated in his flight plan, or a 217° track that would avoid an extensive storm cell. Costello's voice came back: "Thank you, we'll take the 217". The controller instructed the aircraft to "report setting course". The Viscount did not call as expected, and at 1925hr the controller transmitted: "Tango Victor Charlie, have you set course yet?" There was no reply. Further calls also failed to elicit a response so the controller, believing the aircraft had suffered a radio failure, contacted the senior controller to introduce the Uncertainty Phase of a search-and-rescue operation. When no sign of the Viscount could be detected on Sydney's tower radar, this was upgraded to the Alert Phase. The situation was reported to the police, the Royal Australian Air Force (RAAF), Royal Australian Navy (RAN) and the Volunteer Coast Patrol. Coastal shipping was also alerted. Then an air-sea rescue (ASR) launch set out for a night sweep of the foreshores of Sydney's Botany Bay.

It was still possible that the Viscount was continuing in accordance with its flight plan, and in the absence of any reports of an aircraft in trouble the senior controller could do nothing more for the time being. Canberra air-traffic control (ATC) was informed that communication with the Viscount had been lost, and Canberra tower stood by to await its arrival. By 2005hr, the Viscount's estimated time of arrival, there was still no sign of the aircraft. The Distress Phase was introduced, yet still there were no reports of anything suggestive of an accident.

At 2136hr the ASR launch radioed that it had circled Botany Bay without sighting any wreckage. Considering the population density in the area there could be only one inference; VH-TVC had come down in the sea. At first light, aircraft began scouring the open sea off the coast, while a helicopter and motor launches, braving the wild weather, searched the waters of the bay.

At 0630hr the helicopter, investigating an oil slick near the north-eastern shore, sighted what looked like a cushion floating in the water. The ASR launch recovered it, and airline staff identified it as upholstery from the Viscount's cockpit seats.

Meanwhile, searchers checking the north-eastern beaches of Botany Bay came upon small items of cabin furnishings washed ashore, along with human remains. News of the unfolding drama flashed across the nation. It was the first fatal accident involving an Ansett-ANA aircraft in 25 years. In Melbourne a team of investigators, the first of 30, left for Sydney by aircraft.

At about 0830hr RAN divers boarded the ASR launch to check a number of smaller oil slicks on the southern side of the bay. Visibility was poor because of the rain, but presently a police launch drew the divers' attention to an aluminium structure protruding from the water not far away. It was the tip of the Viscount's outer starboard wing. Lying in about 16ft (5m) of water, it bore the registration VH-TVC.

Meanwhile, near the extensive oil slick where the upholstery had surfaced, police divers recovered a bloodstained seat cushion, cabin fabric and human remains. Further upwind the divers found the disintegrated main wreckage, scattered over the seabed in 25ft (7·6m) of water. On the following morning the RAN boom defence vessel *HMAS Kimbla* arrived in Botany Bay, anchoring over the wreckage. For the next four days divers worked hard to recover all the major sections of the wreckage, which was taken to the DCA's hangar at Sydney airport.

The sobering aftermath of the disaster — wreckage of VH-TVC, recovered from the bed of Botany Bay by *HMAS Kimbla*, systematically laid out on the floor of the Department of Civil Aviation's hangar at Sydney Airport.
(Civil Aviation Historical Society/www.airwaysmuseum.com)

Some 85 per cent of Victor Charlie's structure was recovered, including the engines and propellers, and the wreckage examination showed that the starboard outer wing and tailplane components had sustained little impact damage; the remainder of the aircraft had extensively disintegrated.

It became clear that the starboard wing had failed first from aerodynamic overloading, and that the resulting forces on the tailplane caused that component to fail almost simultaneously. The port tailplane, found with the main wreckage, was distorted and bent upwards, showing that this had occurred as a result of aerodynamic loads far in excess of normal. All four engines were running when they struck the water. Calculations based on prop-blade angles indicated that the

aircraft's speed when it hit the water was at least 300kt, and possibly as high as 400kt.

Analysis of the wreckage trail showed the Viscount was on a northerly heading about one mile (1·6km) south of the position of the main wreckage, at between 3,500ft (1,067m) and 5,500ft (1,676m) when it broke up. Residents around Botany Bay reported hearing unusual noises around the time of the accident. Thunder was creating a great deal of noise, but it seemed probable that the noises they heard between 1920hr and 1925hr were either the in-flight break-up or the aircraft hitting the water. The time of the impact was estimated as 1926hr.

So what happened?

At the time of the accident Victor Charlie was fully serviceable and the crew was highly experienced. The only explanation appeared to lie in the violent weather. Indeed, the 29,000-ton P&O Orient liner *Orcades*, Sydney-bound off the coast at the

Grim evidence of the demise of VH-TVC during the investigation; parts of the fuselage have been pieced together on the floor of the hangar in Sydney. The rudder section was not recovered for another 12 years, during which it lay in shallow water on the southern edge of the bay. (Civil Aviation Historical Society/www.airwaysmuseum.com)

time, was battered by a sudden fierce storm soon after receiving a radio message to keep a lookout for wreckage of the missing Viscount. In the USA aircraft had broken up in the extreme turbulence of a squall line, but such destructive conditions had not previously been encountered in Australia's more benign weather.

At the time communication was lost the aircraft would have been about two miles (3·2km) south-east of the airport at a height of around 6,500ft (1,980m), climbing at 165kt (190 m.p.h.). Between this point and the structural failure, something extraordinarily violent happened, causing the Viscount suddenly to lose as much as 3,000ft (915m), increase its speed to perhaps 400kt (460 m.p.h.) and change its heading to northerly. The investigators believed that 'TVC, being flown on instruments, probably encountered a gust of unusual intensity.

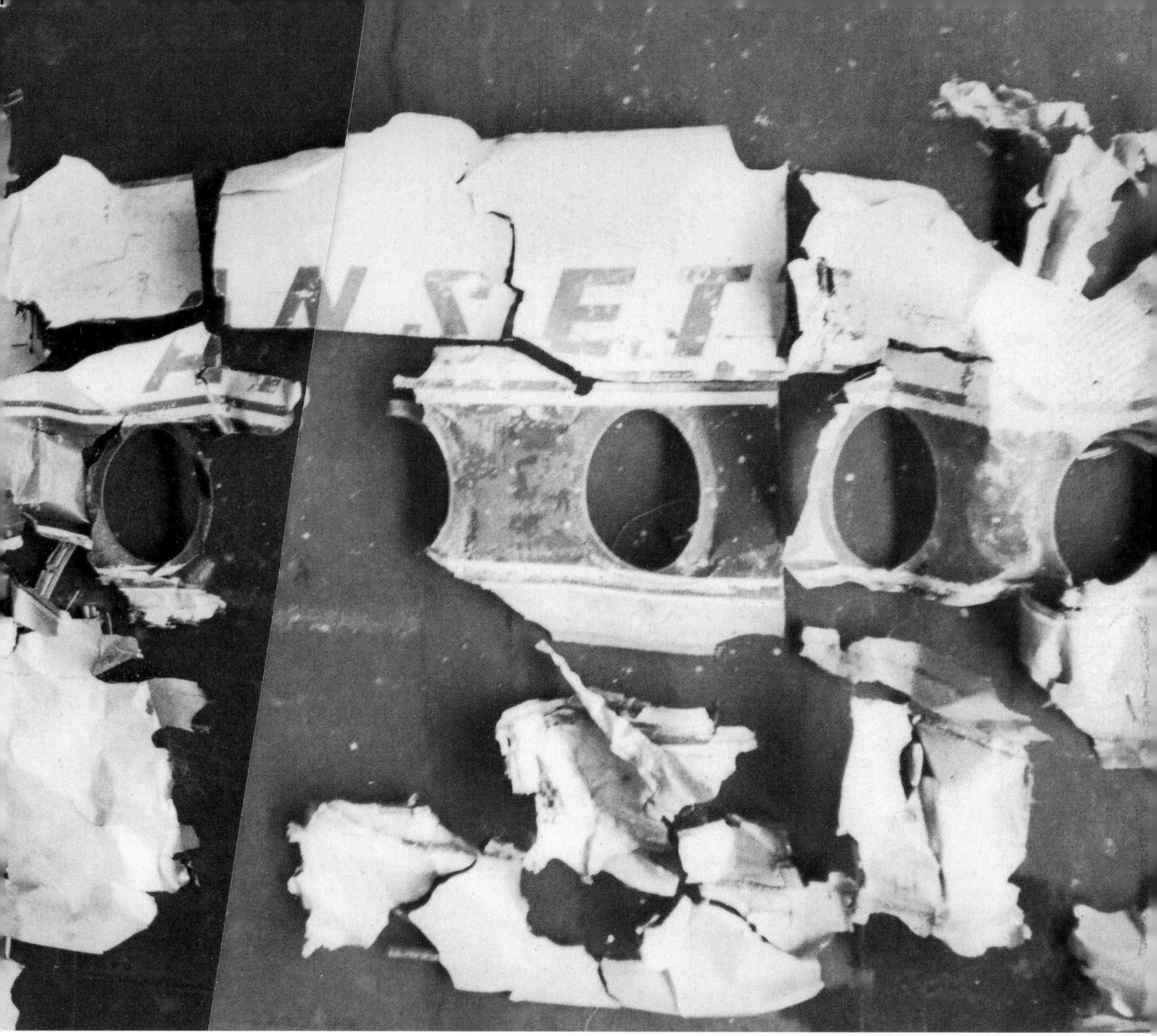

There was a great deal of evidence to support the possibility that that a temporary loss of control resulted from a very severe gust, causing a sudden upset in attitude. With the crew unable to correct it before the aircraft lost substantial height, there would have been a rapid gain in airspeed. The problem would be compounded if the crew's vision was affected by a close lightning flash.

That a modern high-performance airliner in the peak of operating condition, flown by an experienced crew, could so unexpectedly be overtaken by total disaster in a matter of seconds simply because it flew into turbulence in cloud, was profoundly disturbing. Drastic measures were needed to prevent a repetition of the accident.

Airborne weather radar was now available. Qantas Lockheed Constellations were fitted with it, as were the airline's newly-delivered Boeing 707 jetliners. An Air Navigation order was issued requiring all turbine aircraft on the Australian civil register to carry weather radar by June 1, 1963. It was too late to save the crew and passengers of VH-TVC, but the accident led to a significant step forward for commercial aviation safety.

CHAPTER 8

A long career

"Swift, smooth, silent and sure ..."

BY THE TIME the final Viscount order, a batch of six V.843s for the Civil Aviation Administration of China, had left the production line in late 1962, the type had been in service for a decade, with little prospect of a type on the horizon to replace its remarkable profitability on the route-lengths for which it had been designed. George Edwards' original readiness to build an aeroplane tailored to each operator's requirements, as opposed to the American manufacturers' "take it or leave it" attitude, had stood the Viscount in good stead, and Vickers had deservedly reaped the rewards. Ultimately, some 200 individual airlines, companies and organisations in more than 80 countries operated the type over its long and distinguished career, and it is worth taking a look at some of the Viscount's more significant operators.

A luggage label for the BEA Viscount Ulster Flyer service between London and Belfast. (The Aviation Historian Archive)

By far the biggest operator of the Viscount was BEA, which, as launch customer, received the first of its initial order for 20 V.701s in January 1953. The first three were fitted in a first-class-only 40-seat configuration, but the remainder of this initial batch was delivered in a 47-seat five-abreast tourist layout. The first revenue-earning service by a BEA Viscount was flown on April 2, 1953, when G-AMOG flew a freight service from London to Cyprus via Rome and Athens, and the world's first turboprop service to carry fare-paying passengers followed the same route on April 18. By the end of that year BEA's Viscounts were plying their trade on routes from London to destinations as far afield as France, Turkey, Switzerland, Denmark, Sweden, Germany, Italy, Portugal, Scotland and Northern Ireland. The Belfast route was given the name The Ulster Flyer, services to Glasgow and Edinburgh being named The Clansman and Chieftain respectively. Services to Spain commenced in January 1954, and in what must have been a gratifying development for Edwards and Vickers, Viscounts began replacing BEA's Elizabethan class of Airspeed Ambassadors on routes from UK airports to Amsterdam and Paris in the spring of the same year.

BEA's London—Glasgow "luxury air service" was known as The Clansman. (The Aviation Historian Archive)

By mid-1955 BEA's Viscounts were firmly established on their routes, the airline experiencing what would come to be known by the type's order customers as the "Viscount jump", in which the introduction of the type on to a particular service was swiftly followed by a significant increase in passenger traffic on those routes and, importantly, profitability. Utilisation was high, the average day for a Viscount entailing some 8½hr on the line.

This contemporary BEA publicity photograph is a clear demonstration of the number of staff concerned in the operation of one Viscount, including air- and cabin-crew, groundcrew and administrative officers. In the background is V.701 G-AMON, named *RMA Thomas Cavendish*, which was delivered to BEA in March 1954. (Philip Jarrett Collection)

The first production 700-series Viscount, BEA's flagship G-ALWE, named *RMA Discovery*, undergoes engine maintenance in the massive BEA Engineering Base at Heathrow, which was designed to accommodate the airline's Ambassadors (as seen in the background) and Viscounts, and which was completed in 1953. (Philip Jarrett Collection)

Ready to go and with Darts running up, G-ALWF (c/n 5), named *RMA John Franklin*, heads out for a flight during another hardworking day for BEA's Viscount fleet. This aircraft, the world's oldest surviving Viscount, is owned by the Duxford Aviation Society, which maintains it in excellent condition at the Cambridgeshire airfield. (The Aviation Historian Archive)

A contemporary BEA luggage label showing the distinctive planform of the Viscount. (The Aviation Historian Archive)

In February 1954 BEA signed a contract for an initial batch of 12 examples of the stretched and improved 800-series, although such was the airline's faith in the Viscount that another ten V.802s, as BEA's aircraft were designated, were ordered in the spring of 1955, with another two following shortly afterwards. Yet another order was placed in early 1956, this time for 19 Dart 520-powered V.806s, deliveries of which began in 1957. This final order brought the total number of Viscounts purchased by BEA to 70, although others were occasionally drafted in from other operators during times of short capacity.

It was with some fanfare that BEA flew its millionth Viscount passenger on January 18, 1956, a figure that had doubled by the spring of 1957, although the airline was probably less inclined to trumpet its first major Viscount loss, which occurred when G-AMOM was written off during a training accident on January 20, 1956. The same year BEA Viscount services to Venice, Bergen in Norway and the Israeli capital Tel Aviv were opened, the type serving some 53 destinations in Europe, Scandinavia and the Middle East at the peak of BEA's Viscount operations.

Viscount V.701C G-ANHF, named *Matthew Flinders* in BEA service, shares the ramp with a number of BEA DC-3s in the late 1950s. This Viscount (c/n 66) was delivered to BEA in July 1955, and was converted from the standard 40-seat first class or 47-seat tourist layout to a high-density 60/63-seat layout and redesignated as a V.701A. In 1962 it was sold to Brazilian airline VASP and re-registered PP-SRR. Sadly, it crashed into the western slope of Mount Nova Caledonia, near Friburgo, in south-eastern Brazil, on September 4, 1964, killing all aboard. (Mike Hooks)

A classic contemporary BEA publicity photograph showing a member of the aircrew chatting to the passengers over a map in the cabin of a 700-series Discovery-class Viscount (despite clearly still being on the ground!). Note the artwork of Robert Falcon Scott and Ernest Shackleton's three-masted ship *Discovery* on the bulkhead. (The Aviation Historian Archive)

Named *RMA William Baffin* in BEA service, V.701 G-AMOB (c/n 11) became the first Viscount to carry royalty when, on May 14, 1953, the aircraft was used to fly HRH Princess Margaret from London to Fornebu Airport in Oslo for the wedding of Norway's Princess Ragnhild. Seen here at Fornebu, the Viscount flies both the Norwegian and BEA flags from its cockpit while it is refuelled. (Øyvind Munch Ellingsen Collection via The Aviation Historian Archive)

Passengers disembark from BEA V.806 G-APKF (c/n 396), named *RMA Michael Faraday*, at a foggy Heathrow in June 1962. This aircraft was damaged when a BKS Air Transport Ambassador, G-AMAD, crashed on landing at Heathrow on July 3, 1968, substantially damaging a pair of BEA Tridents as it spun out of control towards the uncompleted Terminal 1. The Viscount was quickly repaired, however, and returned to service. (Mike Stroud via The Aviation Historian Archive)

Essentially a beefed-up Viscount with a larger "double-bubble" fuselage and more powerful Rolls-Royce Tyne turboprop engines, the Vanguard was designed to replace the Viscount and offer better economics owing to higher capacity and improved performance. The type became one of the world's fastest turboprops but was to some extent a victim of its time – the dawning of the jet era. (The Aviation Historian Archive)

Passengers board V.806 G-AOYS (c/n 267) at Gatwick during the 1960s. One of 19 ordered by BEA in January 1956, G-AOYS was built at Weybridge and was fitted with Dart 520 engines, and made its first flight on May 23, 1958. Named *RMA George Stephenson* when it was delivered the following month, it is seen here in the "red square" livery introduced by BEA from 1959.
(Philip Jarrett Collection)

As the adventuring fifties turned the corner into the swinging sixties, BEA's hardworking Viscounts, all of which had been delivered by the spring of 1959, were as busy as ever, covering routes as far east as Istanbul, Scandinavia to the north and several locations in North Africa to the south. However, BEA (along with Trans-Canada Air Lines) was still in the market for a faster Viscount of higher capacity, and Vickers accordingly set to work on the Rolls-Royce Tyne-powered Vanguard, which made its first flight in January 1959. The Vanguard was seen as the natural successor to the Viscount, being larger and able to lift twice the load of its predecessor, providing substantially increased profitability. After initial teething troubles, the Vanguard entered BEA service in December 1960, and by the beginning of 1962 the airline had begun to sell off its Viscount 701s, the variant's final revenue service being flown on March 31 that year. Some six million passengers had flown on the airline's 701s over the previous decade. The gap left by the retirement of the lower-capacity V.701s was filled by the 800-series examples, which themselves had been supplanted on the longer routes by Vanguards and de Havilland Comet 4s.

The 800s continued to serve on BEA's routes, although the longer-haul destinations were handed over to the more modern types, Viscounts operating predominantly domestic and short- to medium-haul international services. Several went on to serve with BEA's associated companies, including BKS Air Transport during 1968–69 and Welsh airline Cambrian Airways in 1970, both of which operated V.806s, all 19 of BEA's examples having been integrated into other associated fleets or sold by the end of that year. In April 1971 BEA was restructured into regional divisions, with the remainder of the V.802s being split between BEA Scottish Airways and BEA Channel Islands Airways. The following year 15 of BEA's V.802s were withdrawn from service and subsequently broken

After some ten years in service with BEA as *RMA James Cook*, V.701 G-AMNZ (c/n 20) was acquired by Cambrian Airways in June 1963, when it was painted in the airline's attractive red and white scheme, in which it is seen here at Heathrow in July 1963. It was later leased to Air France during 1967–68 and was eventually withdrawn from service and broken up during 1971. (Mike Stroud via TAH Archive)

up, the airline's jet-powered Hawker Siddeley Tridents and BAC One-Elevens having usurped the Viscount on a number of its European routes. In 1974 BEA was merged with BOAC to form British Airways, which by 1976 had absorbed the BEA-associated Viscount operators, Cambrian and the Scottish and Channel Islands subsidiaries ceasing to exist thereafter. In 1980 it was decided to retire most of the Viscounts, a few remaining on the more remote Scottish services, the last of which was flown on May 8, 1982, bringing to an end some 28 years of service for BEA and its descendants.

Seen here freshly painted in Cambrian Airways' distinctive "orange" livery in 1972, G-AOYG (c/n 256) originally served with BEA from 1958 as *RMA Charles Darwin*, but was acquired by Cambrian in 1970. The colour scheme was short-lived, however, as Cambrian came under control of British Airways in April 1972 and the Viscount had been repainted in BA colours by the summer of 1973. (The Aviation Historian Archive)

Delivered to BEA as *RMA William Murdoch* in honour of the Scottish engineer and inventor in July 1958, G-APEY (c/n 382) served with the airline until April 1968, when it was sold to BKS Air Transport, part of British Air Services, essentially a BEA holding company created to administrate the latter's substantial financial interests in BKS and Cambrian. The aircraft is seen here in January 1969 with BKS markings on its fin and British Air Service titles on the fuselage. It ended its days in Africa in the early 2000s, after having served with British Air Ferries, Air Algerie, Manx Airlines, Virgin Atlantic Airways and several others. (Mike Hooks)

In 1971 BEA was split into regional divisions, each to be given autonomy over how to run its operations. As a result the company's V.802 fleet was divided into two main fleets; one was Scottish Airways based in Glasgow, which operated eight Viscounts. The other was the Channel Islands division, which operated four Viscounts from Jersey, five from Birmingham and one from Guernsey. Both divisions carried BEA's "Speedjack" markings, but with their divisional name beside the BEA logo on the fuselage above the windows. Seen here at Gatwick in April 1971, G-AORD (c/n 171) was allocated to the Channel Islands fleet, with which it remained after its absorption into British Airways in July 1973. (The Aviation Historian Archive)

ABOVE: A gathering of BEA types at Berlin's Tempelhof Airport in June 1969; nearest the camera are 800-series Viscounts G-AOYN (c/n 263) and G-AOHH (c/n 157), with BAC One-Eleven G-AVMJ and de Havilland Comet 4B G-ARJN beyond. (Mike Hooks)

BELOW: Having joined the BEA fleet in June 1958 as *RMA John Harrison*, named in honour of the inventor of the marine chronometer, G-APEX (c/n 381) served the airline until 1969, when it was sold to BKS Air Transport, with which it operated until 1970, when BKS became Northeast Airlines. The latter was subsumed into British Airways in 1974 and G-APEX was put into BA's livery, as seen here at Heathrow in July 1979, until it was withdrawn and stored in 1980. It went on to operate with British Air Ferries during 1981–84 and was eventually broken up for scrap. (Mike Hooks)

One of 12 V.708s ordered in November 1951, F-BGNV (c/n 39) was delivered to Air France in August 1954. In 1962 it was acquired by the French domestic airline, Air Inter, with which it was serving when it was lost in a crash on August 12, 1963. The Viscount crashed into a wood on approach to Lyon, possibly after having been struck by lightning during a severe storm; all four crew and 15 of the 16 passengers, plus one person on the ground, were killed. (The Aviation Historian Archive)

Europe follows suit

Sensing that BEA had picked a winner with its prospective acquisition of the Viscount, Air France placed an order for 12 V.708s in November 1951, the British airline having already begun proving the type in service with the V.630 and V.700 prototypes. The first of Air France's Viscounts was delivered in May 1953, and was configured in a 49-seat layout comprising nine rows of five-abreast and one row of four abreast. The French national carrier's first Viscount services were inaugurated in mid-May 1953 with flights from Paris to Rome and Istanbul, the Viscount replacing the somewhat uneconomical Lockheed Constellation on the latter route.

Air France's V.708s went on to give excellent service throughout the 1950s, the airline experiencing the "Viscount jump" in passenger figures on every route on

Formed in 1954, Lignes Aériennes Intérieures, or Air Inter as it was known, was established to operate domestic services within France and was 25 per cent owned by Air France. Thus it was that when Air France wished to dispose of its V.708 fleet, they would go to Air Inter, the first being delivered in February 1962. By early 1963 the airline was operating a fleet of eight V.708s and the following year four ex-Trans Canada Air Lines V.724s were acquired, including F-BMCH (c/n 50), as seen here. Sadly this aircraft crashed into a mountain on a flight between Lyon and Clermont-Ferrand on October 27, 1972, killing 60 of the 68 people aboard. (Philip Jarrett Collection)

Originally delivered to KLM as V.803 PH-VIH in November 1957, c/n 179 was purchased by Aer Lingus, as were all nine of KLM's fleet of V.803s, in June 1966, when it was registered EI-AOI and given the name *St Fearghal/Fergal*. It is seen here in September 1966 in the airline's smart mid-1960s colour scheme. In 1971 it was leased to British Air Ferries, but by the end of the year it had been withdrawn from use and it was broken up the following year. (Mike Hooks)

An immaculately turned-out Aer Lingus stewardess at the foot of the stairs to one of the airline's V.707s (note the air-conditioning air scoop on the underside of the fuselage and oval doors of the 700-series, which were replaced with rectangular doors on the 800-series). (Philip Jarrett Collection)

which it operated. Only one example was lost in Air France service, when F-BGNK crashed during a training flight on December 12, 1956. Despite offering superb economics and high levels of passenger satisfaction, the Viscount had a comparatively short career with Air France, the introduction of the French-built Sud Caravelle medium-range jetliner in 1959 seeing the beginning of the turboprop's withdrawal. By 1962 Air France had disposed of all of its remaining Viscounts, the majority of which were sold to Air France's associate domestic airline Air Inter, which operated a total of 16 Viscounts until the last few were retired in 1975.

Another European airline quick to see the advantages of the Viscount was Irish national airline Aer Lingus, which became the type's third customer when it ordered four V.707s in November 1951. The first Aer Lingus Viscount service was flown from Dublin to Frankfurt via Manchester and Brussels on April 15, 1954, the airline choosing a 48-seat configuration with two rows of four-abreast and eight rows of five-abreast. Unsurprisingly, the replacement of the company's DC-3s by Viscounts on its services quickly saw a significant increase in passenger numbers and profitability – another

Seen here with the distinctive diagonal-striped tail markings adopted by KLM circa 1960, V.803 PH-VIG (c/n 178), named *Sir Charles E. Kingsford Smith*, taxys in with the outer Darts shut down to save on wear and tear. The aircraft joined the Dutch national airline in November 1957, and in late 1966 was sold to Aer Lingus, with which it became EI-AOM, named *St Feidhlim/Felim*. Sadly, it crashed into the Irish Sea on March 24, 1968, en route from Cork to Heathrow, killing all 57 passengers and four crew aboard. (Mike Hooks)

example of the Viscount jump. As a result, Aer Lingus was swift to order six V.808s when the 800-series became available, in May 1956. Aer Lingus' General Manager, J.F. Dempsey, said at the time: "We have been making an operating profit since we got the Viscount and I have no hesitation in attributing to these aircraft the success we have achieved. We are buying more Viscounts".

The airline's purchase of a fleet of Fokker F-27 Friendship turboprops during 1958-59 left the four original V.707s redundant and these were sold to new owners in 1960. The company acquired two more 800-series Viscounts over the next few years, and in 1966 acquired Dutch airline KLM's entire fleet of nine V.803s. Aer Lingus continued to operate its Viscounts until the end of the 1960s, when jet types, such as the BAC One-Eleven and Boeing 737 joined the fleet. By 1970, Aer Lingus had disposed of its Viscounts.

Cracking North America

While Viscount sales in Europe were gathering pace, George Edwards at Vickers was increasingly aware that for the type to stand a chance of surviving in the global marketplace, it would have to find influential customers in the biggest of all markets, North America. Edwards personally presented the case for the Viscount to Trans-Canada Air Lines (TCAL), and was rewarded with an order for 15 V.724s in November 1952. The Canadians specified some 250 technical modifications, including a redesigned flight deck, the incorporation of more American-furnished equipment, a more powerful heating system and the fitting of Dart 506 engines. Vickers was happy to comply and the order, to the value of $11·5m, was announced as the largest single dollar-earner won by a British company since the war. To add to this victory, Vickers was delighted to receive a further TCAL order for another 36 modified Viscounts, designated V.757s, which were delivered during 1956–59.

The first V.724 arrived in Montreal in December 1954, and after extensive trials, the first North American Viscount service was flown on April 1, 1955, when a TCAL V.724 flew from Montreal to Winnipeg via Toronto and Fort William. By mid-1956 TCAL Viscount services were flying as far east as New York and Boston and as far west as Vancouver. Along with BEA, TCAL was keen to see a larger development of the Viscount, and ordered 20 examples of its successor, the Vanguard, in January

(The Aviation Historian Archive)

ABOVE and BELOW: One of the most important orders for the Viscount came from Trans-Canada Air Lines (TCAL), which ordered 15 examples in late 1952. The airline specified numerous modifications to the standard Viscount to make it suitable for operations in Canada, resulting in the state-of-the-art V.724. This is the first of the TCAL V.724s, CF-TGI (c/n 40), which was given the fleet number "601". (Philip Jarrett Collection)

The first Viscount service to New York was flown from Toronto to Idlewild on April 4, 1955, with thrice-daily Viscount services to the "Big Apple" from Montreal beginning that August. This evocative night shot shows V.724 CF-TGO (c/n 52), fleet number "607", at Idlewild during one of the airline's early Viscount visits. (Philip Jarrett Collection)

1957, which entered service with the Canadian airline in 1960. As a result some of TCAL's Viscounts were disposed of from 1963, the year before TCAL changed its name to Air Canada. The airline's remaining Viscounts continued to serve throughout the 1960s and early 1970s, although the type was gradually confined to shorter routes as the Vanguards took on the longer-range sectors. The final Air Canada Viscount service was flown on April 27, 1974, the majority of the airline's examples being sold on to new owners.

In June 1964 Trans-Canada Air Lines became Air Canada, a name which the company had been using in its French-speaking territories for some time. Accordingly, the Viscount fleet was gradually painted in a new tasteful scheme incorporating a stylised maple leaf on the red fin and a white-top fuselage with a red cheat line. (The Aviation Historian Archive)

The first scheduled turboprop airline service in the USA was performed by a Capital Airlines Viscount on July 26, 1955, and the airline was determined to emphasise the innovative nature of its new airliner, including the type's name on all of its literature, including luggage labels and timetables, as seen here. (David H. Stringer Collection)

The Viscount had also caught the eye of another North American operator, Washington DC-based Capital Airlines, which, after an extended evaluation of the type, placed an initial order for three V.744s in June 1954, with an option for 60 more. American regulations stipulated a number of issues that would have to be addressed to allow the Viscount to fly in the USA, some of which had already been incorporated on the TCAL examples. As a result Vickers incorporated a fuel-jettisoning capability, weather radar, hydraulically-operated integral airstairs and improved heating and air-conditioning equipment, among other modifications, to satisfy the American authorities. Viscounts built to this USA-certificated standard were given a "D" suffix, Capital taking up its option for 60 V.745Ds, as the upgraded examples were designated, in August 1954. Within 11 months, Capital had received the three V.744s and Viscount services commenced on July 26, 1955. Four months later the V.745Ds began to arrive, by which time Capital's promotional department was well into a determined campaign to educate the American public about the advantages of its new fleet of state-of-the-art turboprops. A typical Capital advertisement from the mid-1950s extols the virtues of the sleek British airliner:

"Swift . . . smooth . . . silent . . . sure. The powerful Vickers Viscount introduces the air traveller to an ease and comfort which comes from an almost complete lack of vibration. Unprecedented visibility through large panoramic windows; wide comfortable seats placed only two abreast; perfect air-conditioning and pressurisation . . . all these features combine with the turbine-hushed engines to transform air travel into something more than a race against time."

Despite Capital's resulting uplift in passenger traffic, all was not

Capital took control of every aspect of its Viscount operations, and a comprehensive guide for its employees was issued, which included tips on how to sell the Viscount to potential customers: "Every time you answer the telephone you have an opportunity to deliver an important message about the Capital Viscount; 'May I make a reservation on the Viscount for you' is starting off on the right foot!". (David H. Stringer Collection)

well at the airline financially (and hadn't been since before its acquisition of Viscounts) and an additional order for 15 more V.745Ds in July 1956 ultimately fell through. Capital's comparatively short-route network proved hard to make profitable, despite the arrival of the Viscounts, and by the end of 1958 the airline found itself in difficulties regarding its outstanding repayments to Vickers. In July 1960 it was announced that Capital was to be acquired by United Airlines, and in 1961 the deal was made official. United continued to operate the Viscounts, squaring up financially with Vickers with the allocation of airline shares to the British company among other measures. The Viscounts served on predominantly East Coast and Great Lakes routes

Seen here in Capital's final scheme before the airline was merged with United Airlines in 1961, V.745D N7444 (c/n 200) sits on the ramp at Chicago-Midway alongside a Capital Lockheed Constellation still in the old colour scheme. This Viscount served with United until it was sold to a new owner in California in March 1968, shortly after which it was broken up for spares. (David H. Stringer Collection)

A 1958 Continental Airlines timetable, in which the outer flap announces the "World Premiere of the new and incomparable Jet Power Viscount II". (David H. Stringer Collection)

Vickers test pilot Brian Trubshaw brings V.812 N248V (c/n 360) in to land at the SBAC show at Farnborough in September 1958. Continental lost two Viscounts in accidents. The first, N243V (c/n 354), was on July 8, 1962, when the aircraft settled back on to the runway at Amarillo after the wheels had been retracted on take-off; the pilot lifted the Viscount off the runway but was forced to make a wheels-up landing in a nearby field, with no injuries. The second was N242V (c/n 356) which crashed while landing at Kansas City on January 29, 1963, killing the four crew and five passengers aboard. (The Aviation Historian Archive)

throughout the 1960s, the final scheduled United Viscount service being flown in January 1969.

The second American airline to order Viscounts was Denver-based Continental Airlines, which signed up for 15 examples of the new 800-series straight off the drawing board in December 1955. Continental took delivery of its first V.812 in May 1958, the aircraft being configured in an all-first-class 52-passenger layout with an ingeniously designed interior, which provided an extra 4in (10cm) in cabin width. To differentiate its aircraft from Capital's 700-series examples, Continental promoted its V.812s as "Viscount IIs", a brochure reading: "A glass of water or a cup of coffee will not even ripple as the Viscount II cruises at high speed through smooth air". Once again the Viscount jump made its presence felt, with the airline posting vastly improved traffic figures within six months, despite offering a first-class-only service with the turboprop.

In early 1958 Continental was awarded a significant network expansion, with Texas and New Mexico added to its lucrative Midwest and West Coast routes, all of which were served by Viscounts. Despite the efficiency of the type over Continental's network, the airline entered the jet age when it acquired Boeing 707s from 1959, and the Viscounts gradually had their luxurious interiors replaced with five-abreast all-economy layouts. The 707s also took over most of the airline's longer sectors. By the end of 1967 Continental had disposed of its Viscounts, the majority being sold to UK company Channel Airways, which continued to operate the aircraft in their Continental "Golden Tail" colours, only the legend along the fuselage being replaced with Channel Airways' moniker.

Delivered to Continental Airlines as N244V in June 1958, V.812 c/n 357 was sold to Channel Airways in April 1966 and given the British civil registration G-ATUE. The airline elected to keep the basic Continental livery, only adding Channel Airways titles to the fuselage, and removed the integral airstairs to save weight. Channel ceased operations in February 1972 and its Viscounts were put up for sale, G-ATUE going to Alidair, which never used it and it was broken up in 1977. (Mike Hooks)

The third, and perhaps surprisingly, final American airline to order the Viscount direct from the manufacturer was Boston-based Northeast Airlines, which ordered ten Dart 510-powered V.798Ds in 1957. These ten were in fact part of a batch cancelled by Capital when the latter was experiencing financial difficulty, a situation familiar to Northeast, which shared Capital's frustrations with short-haul routes and their lack of profitability. It was this very problem that prompted the company to acquire Viscounts, which would be far more efficient than the DC-3s, DC-6s and Convairliners it was then operating. The first V.798D was delivered in March 1958

Based in Boston, Massachusetts, Northeast Airlines Inc ordered ten V.798Ds as part of a complicated financial deal with Vickers and Rolls-Royce in July 1957. Delivered to Northeast in August 1958, N6590C (c/n 232) served with the airline until it was repossessed by Vickers in September 1963. The following month it was acquired at auction by Aloha Airlines, which operated it until 1971, when it was sold on to Aeropesca Colombia as HK-1319. It was withdrawn from use at Bogotá in 1982 and broken up for scrap. (The Aviation Historian Archive)

A 1958 promotional item for Northeast Airlines, emphasising the "Jet Prop" aspect of the Viscount. In the event, the airline only operated the type for five years and had to return its examples to Vickers owing to financial difficulties, despite the type's excellent economics. (David H. Stringer Collection)

and all ten were on strength with Northeast by February the following year. Despite the usual jump in traffic resulting from the introduction of the Viscount, which was operated on services down the USA's East Coast as far as Florida, the airline was sinking further into a financial quagmire and Vickers was forced to repossess all nine in 1963 (one had been written off in a non-fatal accident in November 1961). Northeast eventually became part of Delta Airlines in 1972.

Viscount down under

The first non-European airline to order the Viscount was Trans-Australia Airlines (TAA), which placed an initial order for six V.720s in June 1952. The new turboprop offered a high degree of flexibility, which TAA was keen to exploit over its combination of short-sector services between regional centres and transcontinental coast-to-coast routes. The first V.720 was delivered in early October 1954, but unfortunately was lost in a training accident at Mangalore on the 31st of the month, three of the eight aboard being killed. Although the inauguration of the type into scheduled service was delayed by the tragedy, it finally began commercial operations in Australia in December 1954.

The V.720s were fitted with additional fuel tanks in the wings and were the first to incorporate external slipper tanks, to extend the type's range to some 1,380 miles (2,220km). By the spring of 1955 all six V.720s had been delivered, April seeing TAA's 50,000th Viscount passenger carried. Like all airlines that took the

LEFT: The seven V.720s ordered by Trans-Australia Airlines from 1952 were the first Viscounts to be fitted with the auxiliary slipper tanks outboard of the outer Dart engine nacelles, as seen here on VH-TVF (c/n 49). The slipper tanks added a total capacity of 290 gallons to the 1,720–1,900 gallons contained within the four wing tanks, depending on model. (Philip Jarrett Collection)

In January 1959 Trans-Australia Airlines (TAA) ordered two Dart 525-powered V.816s, fitted with a 52-seat + four-seat rear lounge configuration and integral airstairs. Built at Hurn, VH-TVQ (c/n 434) made its first flight on June 8, 1959, and is seen here on a photographic flight before its delivery to Melbourne later the same month. Named *McDouall Stuart* in honour of the 19th-Century Scottish explorer of Australia's interior, the aircraft served with TAA until 1971, when it was acquired by a new owner in Indonesia. (The Aviation Historian Archive)

type on, TAA experienced the Viscount jump after their entry into service, and by May 1956 had ordered seven more, these to be Dart 510-powered V.756Ds, which were delivered during 1956–58. Two Dart 525-powered V.816s were also ordered in 1956, both of which were delivered in 1959.

The second Australian airline to acquire Viscounts was Butler Air Transport (BAT), which served some of the more remote communities in the New South Wales and southern Queensland regions. Two 40-seat Dart 506-powered V.747s were ordered by BAT in June 1954, the first of which arrived in Sydney in early October 1955, the second entering BAT service in September the following year. The Viscounts saw very high utilisation on BAT's routes, although the airline suffered numerous bureaucratic headaches operating from its more isolated outposts,

Still bearing its British registration, G-ANXV, c/n 97 has its starboard Dart 506s run up at Weybridge before its delivery to Australian airline Butler Air Transport, with which it served with the appropriate registration VH-BAT. Named *RMA Warral*, it was delivered to BAT in October 1955 and was transferred into the Ansett-ANA fleet in 1958, when BAT was absorbed into the latter airline. (Philip Jarrett Collection)

some of which were marginal for the type. Following a complex and ultimately successful take-over bid from Ansett Airways as part of its acquisition of Australian National Airways (ANA), BAT and its two V.747s were absorbed into the newly-minted Ansett-ANA conglomerate in 1958. At that time a predominantly DC-6–equipped concern, Ansett-ANA was forced to take on some of TAA's Viscounts as a result of the Airlines Equipment Act of 1958, which called for a degree of standardisation between the nation's two major airlines – whether they wanted it

Viscount VH-RMQ (c/n 45) originally served with Trans-Australia Airlines as VH-TVB, but was acquired and re-registered by Ansett-ANA in November 1962. By 1968 the aircraft had accrued some 30,000 hours of flying time, the first Viscount to do so. It was later leased to MacRobertson-Miller Airlines in 1968, and was lost when one of the wings suffered structural failure during a flight from Perth to Port Hedland on December 31, 1968. All aboard, including 21 passengers, were killed. (John C. Cook via TAH Archive)

or not. In return, TAA was given some of Ansett-ANA's DC-6s, no doubt much to both parties' annoyance. Both airlines continued to operate their Viscount fleets, a mixture of 700- and 800-series aircraft through the late 1950s and 1960s, TAA having withdrawn its examples by mid-1971, Ansett-ANA also having replaced its Viscounts with Douglas DC-9s and Boeing 727s by the end of 1970.

More Viscounts headed for antipodean skies when the New Zealand National Airways Corporation (NZNAC) ordered three V.807s to replace its ageing DC-3s in November 1955. Scheduled NZNAC Viscount services were inaugurated in February 1958, the introduction of the new turboprop swiftly prompting a 40 per cent increase in passenger traffic. The airline had originally intended to use its 800s in a 52-seat configuration with eight spare seats in reserve for peak traffic, but quickly found that it could fill all 60 seats on two round-trips between Auckland and Christchurch every day. In 1961 NZNAC took delivery of another V.807 and acquired a V.804 (designated V.807B) from Polish airline LOT five years later. With the introduction of Fokker F-27s and, later, Boeing 737s, NZNAC began withdrawing its Viscounts from service in 1974, all having been sold on by the end of the following year.

Second-line and corporate operators

More than 70 individual airlines and companies ordered Viscounts direct from the manufacturer, of which only a few of the more significant we have covered in detail here. As the major operators began to replace their Viscount fleets with more modern types, predominantly pure-jet-powered, so a healthy secondhand market developed for a type that still offered exceptional economics for short- and medium-haul operators. By the time the Viscount's long and industrious career

Three Viscounts – N905, N906 and N907 – were ordered by the US Steel Corporation in 1955, designated V.764Ds. The second of these, c/n 184, is seen here at Heathrow during one of several visits to the UK in 1959. The company's trio of Viscounts was used to transport executives and personnel around the USA and internationally, and served the company for some 13 years.
(The Aviation Historian Archive)

As secondhand Viscounts came on to the market as major airlines updated their fleets with jets, so examples were acquired by charter companies meeting the needs of entertainment acts on tour. One musical artist who bought his own Viscount for touring purposes was soul-jazz legend Ray Charles, who purchased ex-Capital Airlines V745D N7445 (c/n 201) in 1968. Re-registered as N923RC, the Viscount, seen here at Pittsburgh in May 1973, was operated by the Ray Charles Organization until 1977. The organisation then acquired ex-Cubana V.818 N500TL, the two Viscounts swapping registrations. (The Aviation Historian Archive)

was over, it had seen service in more than 80 countries, having served nearly 115 separate operators in the UK alone , with 27 airlines and organisations making the most of the Viscount's advantages in Canada and a remarkable 157 American operators having had the type on their books at some point.

It was not only airlines that took an interest in the Viscount; a number of corporate organisations also placed orders direct from the manufacturer. The first

One of the more unusual uses of the Viscount was as a testbed for the Pratt & Whitney Canada PT6A turboprop engine. In November 1972 former Trans-Canada Air Lines V.757 CF-TID (c/n 384) was acquired by the powerplant company and given the experimental-category registration C-FTID-X. Painted in a blue and white colour scheme the aircraft was fitted with a PT6A-50 in its nose, which required substantial strengthening work to the airframe. Tests with various PT6 and PW100-series engines were undertaken during 1974–89, after which it was donated to a museum in Montreal. It moved to a new home in 2011 to serve as a training aid at a firefighting college near Montreal. (Philip Jarrett Collection)

Originally ordered by Howard Hughes in June 1955, the sole V.763D (c/n 82) was built at Hurn, but was transported to Weybridge in March 1956, where it was stored pending final assembly and engine runs to be undertaken by Hughes himself. These never took place, and the aircraft was sold to Central American operator Transportes Aéreos Centro Americanos (TACA) in 1957. In November 1958 the Viscount was delivered to TACA with the El Salvadorean registration YS-09C. It had its career cut tragically short when it crashed on take-off from Managua in Nicaragua on March 5, 1959, killing two of the crew and 13 of the 15 passengers aboard. (The Aviation Historian Archive)

of these was the US Steel Corporation, which ordered three V.764Ds, to be fitted with extra fuel tanks and integral airstairs, in June 1955. All three were delivered to the company during November–December 1956 and served for 13 years before being sold to new owners in 1969.

The next corporate customer to acquire the Viscount was the USA's Standard Oil Corporation, which received its sole V.765D in February 1957. Later that year it became the first Viscount to operate in West Africa. Standard continued to use the aircraft throughout the 1960s and early 1970s, finally selling it off in 1975. The Kuwait Oil Company ordered its Dart 510-powered V.776 in August 1958, this aircraft originally having been built as a V.745D for Capital. It was never

Cuba's national airline operated a total of six Viscounts, the first three V.755Ds being acquired when Cubana took over the contract for the aircraft's original intended customer, Airwork, in late 1955. The V.755Ds — CU-T603, CU-T604 and CU-T605 — began operating from Havana to Miami in May 1956 and domestic routes thereafter, experiencing the "Viscount jump" in full effect. One of the Viscounts, CU-T603, was lost in a hijacking incident in November 1958, and the other two were sold to British Eagle in 1961, when three V.818s were acquired by the airline. The V.818s were sold off in the spring of 1962. (Philip Jarrett Collection)

delivered to the American airline, however, and after brief stints with BEA and Aer Lingus, it was converted to a VIP configuration and operated with British registration G-APNF by British International Air Lines on behalf of the Kuwait Oil Company from late 1958. It was used under complicated leasing arrangements by the corporation until 1962, when it was leased to the Kuwait Airways Corporation. Another undelivered V.745D was acquired by the Royal Bank of Canada in April 1959, the aircraft being designated as the sole V.793D, which operated with the bank until the spring of 1961.

Eccentric billionaire Howard Hughes ordered a V.763D in 1955, to be operated by his company, the Hughes Tool Corporation. The aircraft was substantially completed at Hurn but in 1957 Hughes ordered it to be placed in storage once it had been transported to Weybridge, which it duly was, being covered with sheeting and placed down one side of the Viscount production line. In a typically odd directive from Hughes, Vickers employees were forbidden from removing it from storage or inspecting it in any way. Some two years later Vickers determined to force the issue and the Hughes Tool Corporation gave permission for the Viscount to be inspected. It had deteriorated considerably and some £55,000 would need to be spent to return it to airworthy condition. Hughes lost interest and a deal was brokered in which the aircraft was returned to Vickers, and was later sold to Central American airline TACA International.

As secondhand Viscounts filtered down into the marketplace numerous examples were converted for various uses, including transporting sports teams, music organisations and even religious groups to their destinations, from soul-jazz legend Ray Charles, who purchased an ex-Capital V.745D in 1968 and operated it until 1977, to Rex Humbard, the pioneering American TV evangelist who also used a V.745D to commute to and from his bizarre Cathedral of Tomorrow in Ohio.

Turkish national airline Turk Hava Yollari ordered five Viscounts in July 1957, the first arriving in January 1958. Seen here in the airline's simple but elegant markings, V.794D TC-SEL (c/n 430) joined the fleet in September 1958, serving until June 1971, when it was transferred to the Turkish Air Force, finally retiring in 1996. (Mike Hooks)

One of three ordered by British company Airwork in December 1955, V.755D G-AOCB (c/n 92) was sold before completion to Cubana, with which it served as CU-T604 (see page 103) until 1961, when it was acquired by Eagle Airways (Bermuda), and allocated to Cunard Eagle Airways the following year. After joining Invicta Airways in 1968, G-AOCB was acquired by British Midland Airways as a spares source in 1970. (Mike Hooks)

Part-owned by Alitalia, Somali Airlines received two of the Italian company's V.785Ds during 1968–69. This example, 6OS-AAK (c/n 325) served with Somali until the late 1970s, when it was withdrawn and scrapped. The "S" in the registration was removed on arrival in Somalia. The airline lost the other example, 6O-AAJ (c/n 379) in 1970, and replaced it with V.745D 6O-SAN (c/n 114). (Mike Hooks)

Viscount V.782D c/n 298 was delivered to the Iranian government as EP-AHB in 1958, and was acquired by Central African Airways to become VP-WAT in October 1966. The latter company was dissolved on the last day of 1967 and the aircraft was transferred to Air Rhodesia, in whose colours it is seen here in March 1969. (Mike Hooks)

Former Capital Airlines V.745D N7420 (c/n 118) joined Colombian airline Aerolineas Taxi-Aero Opita (TAO) in November 1968 as HK-1057, having previously operated with Philippine Air Lines (as PI-C773), Hawaiian Airlines (as N745HA) and Alitalia (as I-LIRT). It was withdrawn from use by TAO in 1975 and stored at Bogotá. (The Aviation Historian Archive)

Norwegian shipping group Fred Olsen Lines was an early advocate of the Viscount, taking delivery of four V.779Ds, of which LN-FOH (c/n 250) was one, in April 1957. Named *Otto Sverdrup*, LN-FOH, seen here that year, actually only served the company for a short period, being leased to Austrian Airlines in January 1958, with which it operated until 1960. It was sold in 1962 to Indian Airlines, with which it served as VT-DOE, before joining small Indian airline Huns Air in 1974. (the Aviation Historian Archive)

A good example of the Viscount's longevity and ability to provide sterling service for second-line operators, V.802 G-AOHT, originally built for BEA, is seen here in service with the young Virgin Atlantic Airways in 1985, when it was briefly used for the company's Gatwick—Maastricht route. Its previous operators include BEA, British Airways and British Air Ferries. It was finally retired from BAF service in 1986. (Mike Hooks)

German charter airline Condor Flugdienst leased four of Lufthansa's V.814s, including D-ANOL (c/n 339), during 1964–68, after which it was sold to British Midland to become G-AWXI in 1969. In January 1970 the aircraft suffered an engine fire on take-off from Heathrow and managed to land safely, but was damaged beyond repair. (Philip Jarrett Collection)

Sporting UK airline Northeast Airlines' distinctive yellow-topped colour scheme, V.806X G-AOYO (c/n 264) awaits another flight at Heathrow in the early 1970s. The aircraft served with BEA during 1958–68, after which it joined BKS Air Transport, which became Northeast in 1970. (K.P. Lawrence via The Aviation Historian Archive)

BELOW: Stalwart V.831 G-APND accrued more than 39,000 flying hours during a 24-year career, most of which was spent with British United Airways, but which included stints with Jordanian airline Alia, British Midland, Ghana Airways and and Israeli airline Arkia. It entered service in 1959 and was retired in 1983. (Philip Jarrett Collection)

CHAPTER 9

Survivors

Delivered as a V.757 to Trans-Canada Air Lines with fleet number "627" in May 1957, CF-THI (c/n 270) was absorbed into the Air Canada fleet in 1964, and served with the airline until 1969, having been used for an average of more than six hours a day during its 12-year career. After preservation work by Air Canada, the aircraft was flown to Rockcliffe, Ottawa, on November 18, 1969, the day after which it was officially handed over to Canada's National Museum of Science & Technology, where it spent most of its time outdoors, as seen here. In January 2000 the museum was renamed the Canada Aviation Museum, and in 2006 the Viscount was moved into the museum's storage facility, where it remains in one piece standing in its own undercarriage. The museum was renamed again in 2010 as the Canada Aviation & Space Museum. (The Aviation Historian Archive)

Following its 18-year career with BEA, Channel Airways, British Eagle and Cambrian Airways, the second V.701, G-ALWF (c/n 5), was acquired by the Viscount Preservation Trust in April 1972 with a view to preserving it and putting it on public display at Speke Airport in Liverpool. In February 1976 the Viscount was trucked to Duxford, Cambridgeshire, where it was to be restored by Duxford Aviation Society, which acquired the airliner on loan for a period of 99 years. During 1984–85 its Cambrian Airways markings were badly faded so it was restored to its original BEA livery, as seen here. It was re-restored in the same markings in 2005, and remains on display at Duxford in 2017. (The Aviation Historian Archive)

VICKERS VISCOUNT SURVIVORS

By some margin Britain's most successful post-war airliner, a number of complete Viscount airframes, as well as significant sections of individual aircraft, still survive in various locations around the world. The list below is presented in order of airframe construction number (c/n). All are complete airframes unless otherwise noted.

C/n	Reg/serial	Variant	Owner/Location
5	G-ALWF	V.701	Duxford Aviation Society, Imperial War Museum Duxford, UK
7	G-AMOG	V.701	National Museum of Flight, East Fortune, Scotland, UK
35	F-BGNR	V.708	Midland Air Museum, Baginton, Coventry, UK
38	F-BGNU	V.708	Auto und Technik Museum, Sinsheim, Germany
40	CF-TGI/N22SN	V.724	Pima Air & Space Museum, Tucson, Arizona, USA
54	CF-TGQ/F-BMCF	V.724	Institute Aéronautique Amaury de la Grange, Lille, France
64	G-ANHD/PP-SRO	V.701C	Museu Eduardo André Matarazzo, São Paulo, Brazil
144	CF-TGZ/N3832S	V.757	Commemorative Air Force, Rio Grande Valley Wing, Brownsville, Texas, USA
148	VH-TVJ	V.756D	Nose section only. Queensland Air Museum, Caloundra, Queensland, Australia
161	G-AOHL	V.802	Nose section only. Mayhem Paintball Centre, Abridge, Essex, UK
213	N7458	V.745D	Forward fuselage and nose section only. Wings of History Museum, San Martin, California, USA
224	CF-THG	V.757	British Columbia Aviation Museum, Sidney, BC, Canada
233	N7471	V.745D	Mid Atlantic Air Museum, Reading, Pennsylvania, USA. Also registered as N6591C, N820BK, N1898T and N98KT during career
248	G-AOXU	V.804	Nose section only. Aeropark, East Midlands Airport, Leicestershire, UK. Also registered as SP-LVC, ZK-NAI, VQ-GAB and G-CSZB during career
263	G-AOYN/G-OPAS	V.806	Nose section only. Bournemouth Aviation Museum, Hurn, Dorset, UK
270	CF-THI	V.757	Canada Aviation & Space Museum, Ottawa, Ontario, Canada
279	CF-THS	V.757	Royal Aviation Museum of Western Canada, Winnipeg, Manitoba, Canada
283	ZK-BRF	V.807	Ferrymead Aeronautical Society, Christchurch, New Zealand
318	VH-TVR	V.818	Australian National Aviation Museum, Moorabbin, Melbourne, Victoria, Australia. Also registered as CU-T622 and ZS-CVB during career
339	D-ANOL/G-AWXI	V.814	Nose section only, underwater. National Diving Centre, Stoney Cove, Leicestershire, UK
345	FAB 2101/C-90 2101	V.789D	Força Aérea Brasileira Museu Aeroespacial, Rio de Janeiro, Brazil
346	ZS-CDT/G-AZLP	V.813	Nose section only. Brooklands Museum, Weybridge, Surrey, UK
350	ZS-CDX/G-AZNA	V.813	Kokorico discotheque, Waarschoot, Belgium
368	D-ANAM	V.814	Flugausstellung Aviation Museum, Hermeskeil, Germany
369	D-ANAB	V.814	Flugzeug Restaurant Silbervogel, Hanover, Germany
371	9G-AAV/XT661	V.838	Nose section only. Bruntingthorpe, Leicestershire, UK
375	SE-IVY	V.815	High Chapparal AB Wild West Theme Park, Kulltorp, Sweden. Also registered as AP-AJF and G-AVJB during career
384	CF-TID/C-FTID-X	V.757	Institut de Protection Contre les Incendies du Québec, Canada
412	G-APIM	V.806	Brooklands Museum, Weybridge, Surrey, UK
430	TC-SEL/430	V.794D	Havacilik Muzezi air museum, Istanbul, Turkey
438	XT575	V.837	Nose section only. Brooklands Museum, Weybridge, Surrey, UK. Also registered as OE-LAG and LZ-BEO during career
447	D-ANAF	V.814	Technik Museum Speyer, Heidelberg, Germany
453	50258	V.843	China Aviation Museum, beijing, China. Also registered as G-ASDS, 406 and B-406 during career

CHAPTER 10 Viscount colours Artworks by Juanita Franzi

The artworks presented here are to scale with each other.

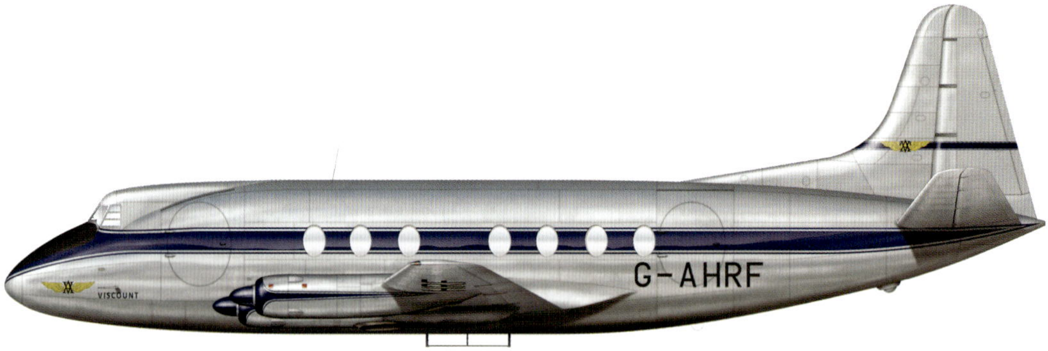

The sole V.630 prototype (c/n 1), registered G-AHRF, made its first flight on July 16, 1948, and is seen here in the colours in which it appeared at the SBAC Show at Farnborough in September that year. Finished in a standard aluminium paint with dark blue trim, the aircraft carried Vickers' golden-wing insignia on the nose and fin, and the word "Viscount" on the forward fuselage. The V.630 was given the military serial VX211 and RAF roundels in October 1948 for trials work, before reverting to its civil registration in August 1949. After extensive testing, the aircraft was written off after a landing accident in Sudan on August 27, 1952.

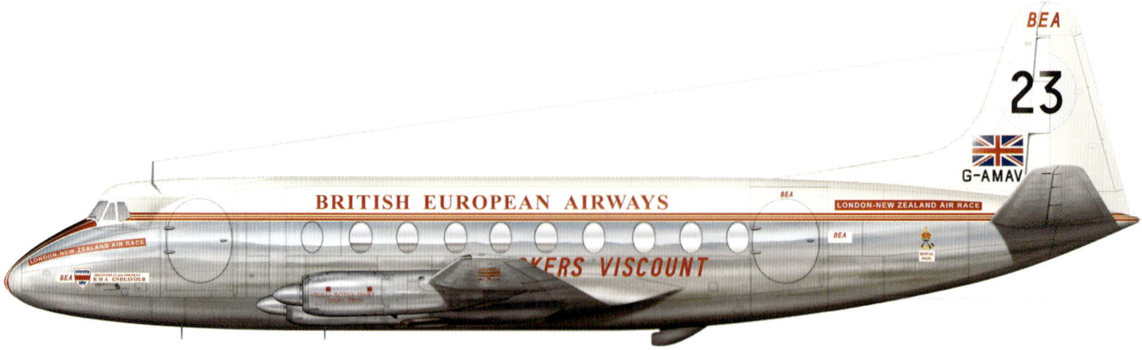

Seen here wearing the markings it carried for the 1953 London—New Zealand Air Race, G-AMAV (c/n 3) was the prototype Viscount V.700, which made its maiden flight on March 15, 1950. Although G-AMAV was owned by the Ministry of Supply, authority was given to Vickers to operate it on a series of demonstration flights and route-proving flights, and in 1953 the aircraft was selected to participate in the air race between the UK and New Zealand — see page 30 — for which it was painted in BEA markings (including the name *RMA Endeavour*) and given the race number "23", along with a special nose legend and the words "Vickers Viscount" displayed prominently on the fuselage. Used extensively for trials and demonstration flights, G-AMAV made its last flight on April 1, 1958, the fuselage being donated to the Stansted Fire School in August 1963.

Viscount V.707 EI-AGI (c/n 34) was one of four initially ordered by Irish national airline Aer Lingus in November 1951, and made its maiden flight on March 24, 1954. Delivered the following month with the name *Saint Lorcán O'Tuathail / St Laurence O'Toole* (a 12th-Century Archbishop of Dublin), the aircraft was painted in the airline's standard natural metal finish with green and white trim lines. The "green top" scheme seen here was introduced in late 1955, and incorporated a Winchester Green upper fuselage and English Green cockpit section. The rudder was white, as was the cheat line into which the windows were set. This Viscount remained with Aer Lingus until April 1959, when it was withdrawn from service, and continued its career with Tradair as G-APZC. It was finally scrapped at Southend in 1970.

The first Viscount V.708 to be delivered to Air France, F-BGNK (c/n 8) joined the airline in May 1953. On December 12, 1956, this Viscount departed Paris (Orly) and climbed to 3,000ft (915m) during a training flight to Reims. The aircraft was cleared to 5,000ft (1,524m) before being seen to suffer from a loss of control and diving into the ground at Dannemois, near Orly airport. All five crew members aboard were killed. The aircraft is seen here in the airline's handsome standard 1950s scheme, the only change being the incorporation of larger letters for the "Air France" legend from 1955.

Viscount V.720 VH-TVC (c/n 46), named *John Oxley*, arrived in Australia in December 1954 as part of an order for six placed by Trans-Australia Airlines (TAA), with which it served until March 1960. Under the provisions of Australia's "Two-Airline Policy", VH-TVC was leased to rival company Ansett-ANA in March 1960 and painted in the latter's scheme, which comprised a simple fin marking bearing the legend "Viscount" and the registration. The colour scheme was later revised to incorporate the fin markings with the airline's titles, as seen here. On November 30, 1961, VH-TVC took off from Kingsford Smith Airport, Sydney, in a severe thunderstorm, bound for Canberra. It suffered structural failure and crashed into Botany Bay – see pages 72–79 for the full story.

One of the most important early Viscount customers was Trans-Canada Air Lines (TCAL), which ordered 15 V.724s in November 1952. The first of TCAL's Viscounts — and the first of the type to be delivered to a North American operator — CF-TGI (c/n 40) arrived in Winnipeg in December 1954. The aircraft wore the attractive TCAL scheme in which it is seen here until 1957, when the fin and top of the cabin were painted white. Making its final TCAL flight in January 1963, CF-TGI was leased to Transair (Canada), with which it served until 1971. The aircraft was operated by a number of American operators as N22SN during the 1970s and 1980s, and was finally withdrawn from service in 1987. It is currently on display at the Pima Air & Space Museum in Tucson, Arizona.

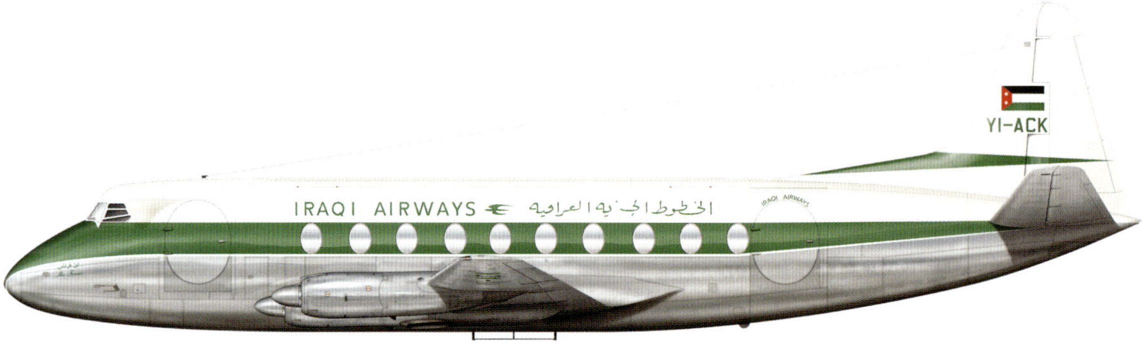

The first Viscount V.735 to be delivered to Iraqi Airways, YI-ACK (c/n 67) is seen here in the colour scheme it wore when it entered service with the airline in October 1955, before it was fitted with weather radar in 1957. First flown on September 23, 1955, YI-ACK was named *Ibn Firnas* in honour of the 9th-Century Islamic Iberian scholar and scientist and served with Iraqi Airways until 1978, when it was acquired by Alidair and registered as G-BFMW. It also briefly operated on lease to Southern International, Guernsey Airlines and Air UK before being withdrawn from use in January 1982 and used for fire practice.

Originally operated as N7403 by Capital Airlines from July 1955 until February 1958, when it was briefly used for training by Continental Airlines before being returned to Vickers, Viscount V.744 c/n 89 operated under lease to Japanese airline All Nippon Airways as G-APKK during 1960–61. In January 1962 it was purchased by the UK Ministry of Aviation, given the military serial XR801 and allocated to the Empire Test Pilots School (ETPS) at Farnborough (Boscombe Down from January 1968). The aircraft served with the ETPS until October 1971, when it was sold to Shackleton Aviation Ltd, which had it flown to Coventry (Baginton) in May 1972, after which it was scrapped.

Representing a turning point for Vickers in terms of sales of the Viscount, Capital Airlines operated more than 60 examples of the type, including V.745D N7447 (c/n 203), the 46th Viscount ordered by the airline. Making its first flight at Hurn on October 22, 1956, N7447 was delivered to Capital, complete with integral "airstairs", seven days later, when it was given the Capital fleet number "366". It was later fitted with weather radar, but is seen here in the colours it wore on delivery. The registration was removed from the fin circa 1958 and applied in larger letters on the rear fuselage, in line with newly-introduced FAA requirements. The aircraft became part of United Air Lines' fleet when the latter acquired Capital during 1960–61, United operating it until January 1968, when it was withdrawn and broken up for scrap.

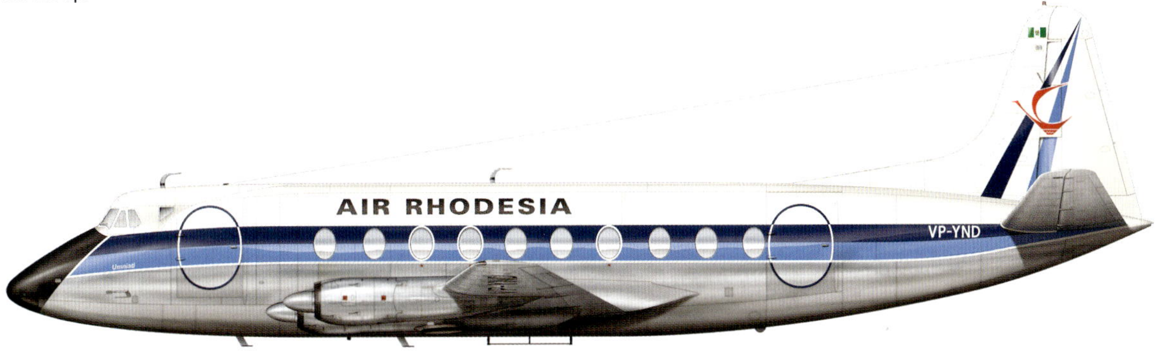

In July 1954 Central African Airways (CAA), established in 1946 by the governments of Northern Rhodesia, Southern Rhodesia and Nyasaland, ordered five Viscount V.748Ds fitted with weather radar. One of these was VP-YND (c/n 101), which had been rolled out early and been used to return a British aircraft industry delegation from Moscow in June 1956, making it the first Viscount to visit the Soviet Union. The aircraft was delivered to CAA the following month, named *Mweru*. The airline was dissolved in December 1967 and VP-YND passed to the newly-formed Air Rhodesia, with which it was renamed *Umniati*. It is seen here in the colours it wore circa 1975. On February 12, 1979, VP-YND was shot down shortly after take-off from Salisbury by a pair of Strela surface-to-air missiles fired by nationalist guerillas; all 59 passengers and crew aboard were killed.

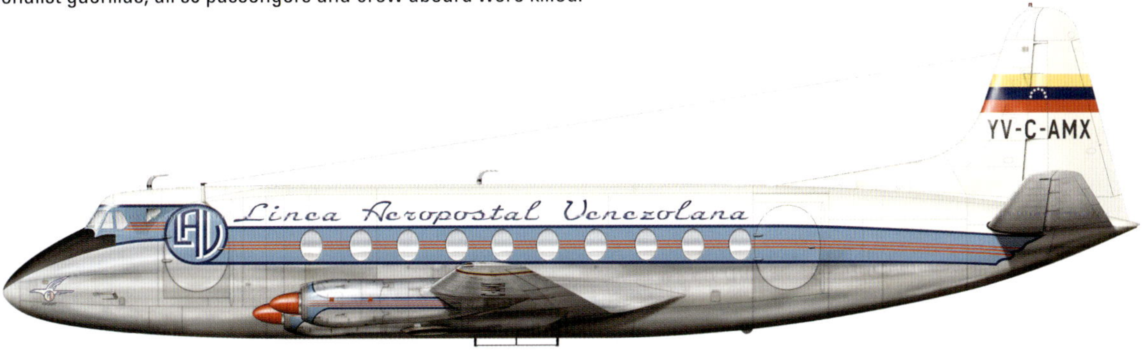

Viscount V.749 YV-C-AMX (c/n 95) was one of three 40-seat Dart 506-powered examples ordered by Venezuelan carrier Linea Aeropostal Venezolana in May 1954. Making its maiden flight on February 8, 1956, the aircraft was delivered the following month and is seen here in the colourful scheme it carried during the late 1950s and early 1960s. On August 14, 1974, YV-C-AMX crashed into a mountain on the Venezuelan island of Margarita during a tropical storm, killing all aboard.

Named *George Bass* in honour of the 18th-Century British naval surgeon and explorer of Australia, V.756D VH-TVH (c/n 146) was one of a total of seven ordered by Trans-Australia Airlines (TAA) in April 1955. Powered by four Dart 510s and arranged in a 44-seat configuration, VH-TVH was delivered to TAA in June 1956, the same month it set a new civil aviation speed record for its class when it flew from Melbourne to Launceston in 51min. Three months later it set a new record on the Melbourne—Adelaide service, completing the flight in 1hr 9min 30sec. It is seen here in TAA's attractive early 1960s colour scheme. The aircraft flew its last commercial flight in December 1968 and was scrapped in mid-1970.

Norwegian shipping and airline company Fred Olsen Flyselskap's relationship with the Viscount began with the delivery of a pair of V.736s in late 1955. In 1957 four more Viscounts were ordered, this time V.779Ds, one of which was LN-FOM (c/n 247), which was leased to Austrian Airlines as OE-LAE during 1958–60, and as G-ARBW to BEA from June 1960 to January 1961. After a very brief return to Fred Olsen it was then leased to Scandinavian Airline System for most of the rest of 1961. It is seen here in the Fred Olsen scheme in which it was delivered to the company in 1957. In 1962 it was sold to Indian Airlines, with which it operated as VT-DOD until 1971, when it was withdrawn from use and broken up.

Seen here in the stylish colours of Italy's national airline Alitalia circa mid-1960s, V.785D I-LIFE (c/n 325) was originally delivered to Linee Aeree Italiane (LAI), which ordered six 700-series Viscounts in May 1956, with another order for four following on in January 1957. In August that year LAI and Alitalia merged, the latter keeping the name and LAI's Viscounts being repainted in Alitalia colours. This aircraft overran the runway on landing at Alghero on August 1, 1958, but there were no casualties and the aircraft was repaired. In 1969 I-LIFE was sold to Somali Airlines, with which it was registered as 60S-AAK (60-AAK from June 1969). It was withdrawn from use at Mogadishu in 1977 and broken up.

A relatively simple but attractive colour scheme was worn by the V.794Ds of Turkish national airline Turk Hava Yollari, which ordered four examples of the Dart 510-powered variant in July 1957. This aircraft, TC-SEV (c/n 429), was delivered on August 1, 1958, but had served for little more than six months when it crashed on approach to Gatwick Airport on February 17, 1959, with Turkish Prime Minister Adnan Menderes aboard on his way to sign a treaty over Cyprus in London. Nine of the 16 passengers aboard were killed but Menderes survived. The accident was due to the combination of poor weather and an incorrectly-set or misread altimeter.

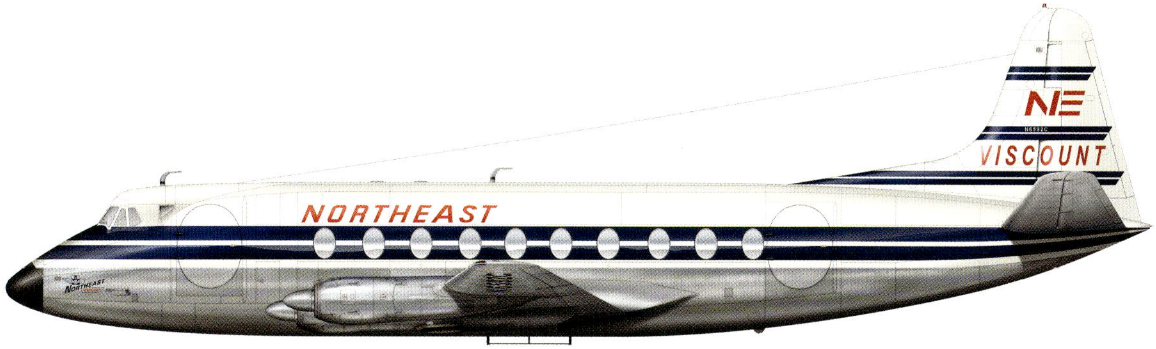

Only three American airlines ordered Viscounts direct from the manufacturer; Capital, Continental and Boston, Massachusetts-based Northeast Airlines, the latter ordering ten V.798Ds in 1957 for its somewhat uneconomical short-sector routes. Delivered to Northeast in August 1958, N6592C (c/n 234) served with the airline until it was damaged beyond repair at Boston's Logan Airport on November 15, 1961, when a departing Douglas DC-6B of National Airlines tore off the Viscount's tail and outer section of the port wing after commencing take-off without clearance. Miraculously, there were no serious casualties among the Viscount's eight crew and 37 passengers or the 30 passengers and crew aboard the DC-6B.

Built at Weybridge and first flown there in February 1957, V.802 G-AOHH (c/n 157) joined the British European Airways (BEA) fleet the following month in the airline's "Three Crown" colour scheme, with the name *Sir Robert McClure* (after the 19th-Century Irish Arctic explorer). The stylish but restrained "Red Square" scheme in which it is seen here was introduced by BEA in 1959; aircraft were repainted only as they came up for major overhauls, so there was often a gap between the official introduction of a scheme and its application to individual aircraft. For example, the later "Speedjack" scheme created by Henrion Design Associates was unveiled in August 1968, but G-AOHH retained the "Red Square" until 1970. In April 1971 the aircraft was allocated to BEA Scottish Airways and again to British Airways (European Division) in 1973. In 1975 G-AOHH was withdrawn from service and after all useable parts had been removed was ignominiously moved to the fire dump at Leeds.

Boasting one of the longest careers in the type's history, Viscount V.806 G-AOYJ (c/n 259) was one of 19 ordered by BEA in 1956, and made its first flight on December 9, 1957. Delivered in January 1958 G-AOYJ served with BEA until it was leased in October 1965 to Cyprus Airways, spending the next five years with the latter before being taken on strength by Cambrian Airways, part of British Air Services, a subsidiary of BEA, in November 1970. In 1973 Cambrian was absorbed into British Airways (BA), G-AOYJ joining the latter's fleet. By 1976 the distinctive BA livery designed by Negus & Negus in 1974 had been applied and the aircraft is seen here circa 1980, the year before it was withdrawn from use and stored. It went on to serve with other airlines, however, until its final retirement in 1993.

Built at Weybridge, Dart 525-powered V.806 G-AOYH (c/n 311) made its first flight on October 25, 1957, before being delivered to the airline in December that year as *William Harvey*. In 1964 G-AOYH was one of six V.806s modified to incorporate the high-density seating configuration and Dart 510s of the V.802 and redesignated V.806Xs. In July 1968 the aircraft was allocated to BKS Air Transport, which in November 1970 became Northeast Airlines, in whose colours the aircraft is seen here circa 1972. The aircraft was re-allocated to British Airways (Regional Division) in 1976, for which it flew its last service in March 1982. After periods with British Air Ferries and Canadian operator North Cariboo Flying Service (as C-GWPY) and Euroair Transport Ltd (as G-BNAA), it was withdrawn from use in May 1987 and broken up at Southend in 1991.

The first of 15 Dart 525-powered V.812s ordered by Continental Airlines in December 1955, N240V (c/n 353) made its first flight on February 14, 1958, and was delivered to the airline that May. This aircraft, named *Los Angeles*, had a comparatively short career with Continental and was acquired by the Tennessee Gas Transmission Corp in August 1960, when it was re-registered as N501T (N501TL from 1973). In 1975 the aircraft was sold to Alidair, which operated it in the UK (and leased it to Cyprus Airways during March–May 1976) until it was sold to Chinese company Far Eastern Air Transport and re-registered B-2037 in September 1976. Leased to Indonesian carrier Mandala Airlines as PK-IVS during 1976–79, it retained that registration when leased to Bouraq Indonesia Airlines in 1980. Sadly, the aircraft crashed near Jakarta on August 26, 1980, killing all aboard.

Originally built as a Dart 525-powered V.815 for Pakistan International Airlines (PIA), c/n 375 first flew on August 15, 1959, and entered PIA service as AP-AJF (named *City of Karachi*). In 1967 the aircraft was sold to Hawker Siddeley and given the British registration G-AVJB. Operating with British Midland Airways (BMA) and Nigeria Airways under lease, it was purchased by BMA in May 1969 and spent the next ten years operating with numerous carriers including Kestrel International Airways, Alidair, Cyprus Airways and Intra Airways (Jersey European Airways from 1979), which bought the aircraft in 1976. After brief periods in storage the aircraft, christened *Jane,* was acquired in September 1981 by British Air Ferries, in the colours of which it is seen here circa 1983, when it was again put into storage. In late 1986 it was purchased by Swedish operator Baltic Airlines, which operated it until April 1989. It was then donated to the High Chapparal theme park near Kulltorp in Sweden. It suffered fire damage in 1992 but was repaired and remains on display.

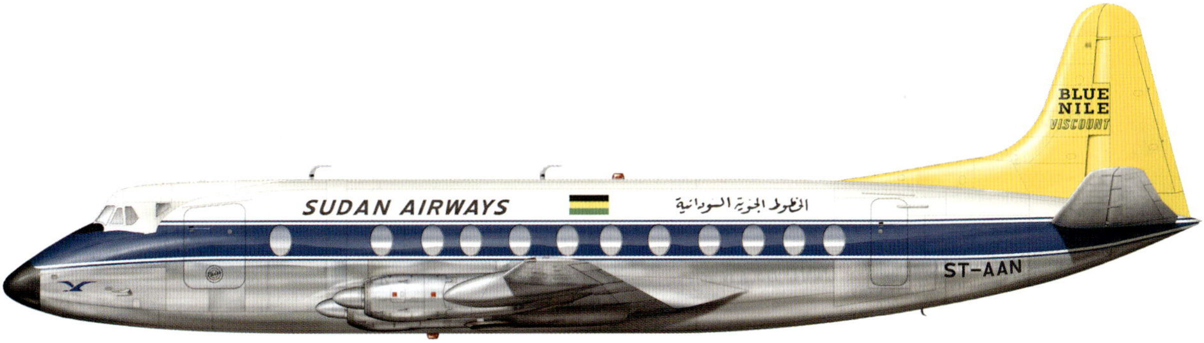

Initially ordered by Airwork Ltd in early 1958, V.831 ST-AAN (c/n 419) was leased immediately on delivery in June 1959 to Sudan Airways, serving as the airline's only Viscount. Powered by four Dart 530s and incorporating removable "slipper" fuel tanks on the wings outboard of Nos 1 and 4 engines, as seen here, the aircraft inaugurated the airline's "Blue Nile" service from Khartoum to London via Athens and Rome, and was also used on the Beirut and Asmara routes, all operated by Airwork crews. In 1962 the aircraft was registered G-ASED for use by British United Airways (BUA), and was used in 1965 by Spanish airline Aviaco as EC-AZK. After serving with BUA as G-ASED, it joined the British Midland fleet in 1967 and was sold on again to Alidair in 1972. Two years later the aircraft was acquired by Israeli airline Arkia and registered 4X-AVG, as which it was finally retired in May 1982 and broken up at Tucson, Arizona.

One of four Dart 525-powered V.832s ordered by Ansett-ANA in May 1958, VH-RMI (c/n 416) made its first flight on April 8, 1959, and was delivered from the UK to Melbourne during April 24–29 that year. Initially carrying the airline's standard markings with a blue strip on the red fin bearing the legend "Viscount II", VH-RMI is seen here with the revised fin scheme introduced in late 1962/early 1963. On September 22, 1966, this aircraft was en route from Mount Isa to Brisbane, Queensland, when a fire in one of the cabin pressurisation blower units spread to the wing tank and Nos 1 and 2 engines, causing a catastrophic failure of the port wing spar. The Viscount crashed near Winton, Queensland, killing all on board.

In April 1960 Ghana Airways ordered three V.838s, to be powered by Dart 525s. The first to be delivered was 9G-AAV (c/n 371), in October 1961. In February 1965 it was sold to the UK's Ministry of Technology, acquiring the RAF serial XT661. Allocated to the Radar Research Establishment at Pershore, the Viscount was fitted with electronic equipment in various fuselage-mounted pods for extensive radar and signals trials. When it was transferred to the RAE at Thurleigh in 1977, the original blue and white scheme was replaced with the "raspberry ripple" scheme seen here, retaining these colours after its move to the Royal Signals & Radar Establishment at RAE Bedford in 1979. Making its final flight in February 1989 it was withdrawn from use and stored outside at Thurleigh. In 1993 the aircraft was acquired by Texas-based International Turbine Service, which, after removing the Dart 525s, left the airframe to be broken up by a local company.

The finishing touches are applied to Transair V.804 G-AOXU (c/n 248) at the Vickers factory at Weybridge in 1957. Typical of the type's longevity, this machine went on to serve with more than ten different operators over a career that spanned nearly four decades, from its first flight in August 1957 to its last in October 1996. (The Aviation Historian Archive)

Acknowledgments

THE PREPARATION OF this book would have been impossible without the considerable assistance and expertise of numerous individuals, all of whom gave generously of their time and resources, and to whom I owe a great debt of gratitude. My thanks go to contributors Philip Jarrett, the late Mike Hooks, Steve Greensted and the late John Havers and John Cook, whose photographs have added so much to this volume, and to the ever-dependable Juanita Franzi of Aero Illustrations, who has provided the magnificent artworks for it. I am extremely grateful to Esma Job and Alexandra Sasse, widow and daughter respectively of the late Macarthur Job, who wrote the splendid section on the crash of Viscount VH-TVC. I am also profoundly indebted to Phil Vabre of Melbourne's Airways Museum / Civil Aviation Historical Society, about which more may be found at www.airwaysmuseum.com. As always, much-appreciated encouragement and advice, as well as excellent memorabilia, came from David H. Stringer, History Editor at American magazine AIRWAYS, and I am also grateful to Fred Crosskey and Capt Dacre Watson for their invaluable efforts on my behalf.

A number of sources were of great help when putting this book together, including Air-Britain's exhaustive chronicle and production list of the Viscount by Rayner G.C. Kittle; also *Viscount, Comet & Concorde; Legends of the Air Vol 3* (Aerospace Publications Pty Ltd, 1996) by Stewart Wilson, Editor of premier

A British United Viscount undergoes an engine change at Gatwick airport. The combination of British airframe know-how coupled with cutting-edge British engine technology made the Viscount a world-beater — and the best-selling British airliner of all time.
(The Aviation Historian Archive)

Australian aviation magazine *Aero Australia*; honourable mentions are also in order for *Classic Civil Aircraft Vol 4: Vickers Viscount* by Alan J. Wright (Ian Allan, 1992) and *The Brabazon Committee and British Airliners* by Mike Phipp (Tempus, 2007). All are first-rate and are recommended for readers who want to dig further into various aspects of the Viscount story.

Acknowledgment must also be made to the excellent Viscount.net, the definitive online resource and "virtual museum" maintained by a global network of Viscount enthusiasts whose work, unlike much of what may be found on the internet, is unfailingly reliable and authoritative. (www.vickersviscount.net)

Sincere thanks are also due to Mick and Lynn Oakey, two of my three partners at *The Aviation Historian*, for their continuing support, as well as to the third partner, my long-suffering wife Amanda, who now knows far more than she ever wanted to about the Viscount. And last but by no means least, I offer my profound thanks, apologies and sympathies to Martin Mace, without whose vision, support and forbearance this book would have been impossible.